A Thrill of
HOPE

An Advent Devotional

 *Look up, you whose gaze is fixed on this earth, who are spellbound by the little events and changes on the face of the earth. Look up to these words, you who have turned away from heaven disappointed. Look up, you whose eyes are heavy with tears and who are heavy and who are crying over the fact that the earth has gracelessly torn us away. Look up, you who, burdened with guilt, cannot lift your eyes. Look up, your redemption is drawing near. Something different from what you see daily will happen. Just be aware, be watchful, wait just another short moment. Wait and something quite new will break over you: God will come.*

—**Dietrich Bonhoeffer**
God Is in the Manger

A Thrill of
HOPE
at a Glance

Each **SUNDAY OF ADVENT** introduces the week's theme.

Each **WEEKLY PRAYER** draws from ancient hymns or prayers.

COME TO THE TABLE invites you to gather together in community for a meal, preferably on Sundays, whether among family or friends. Each Sunday contains a short reflection and discussion questions to share with the group. Suggested memory verses are provided to help bring the weekly theme and scripture to life.

The **DAILY DEVOTIONAL REFLECTIONS,** meant to be read throughout the week, have been written by various storytellers, leaders, and pastors.

The **DAILY READINGS** of Scripture are based on Year C of the Revised Common Lectionary.

The Anticipation of
HOPE

First Sunday of Advent

DECEMBER 2, 2018

Weekly Prayer

God of our waiting time,
with the holy ones who have gone before us,
we long once more for the coming of Jesus,
your Word made flesh.

Utter your Word anew in our world
at once beautiful and wounded.

Open our hearts to listen for your voice
as the human family cries out
for justice and hungers for meaning.

Wait with us, accompany us,
work and pray through us for the unfolding
of your promise, for the fullness
of your dream this Advent and always.

—Sister Christine Koellhoffer

MEMORY VERSE CHALLENGE

Heaven and earth will disappear, but my words will never disappear.
—Luke 21:33 (NLT)

Come to the Table

SUNDAY SCRIPTURE READING
Luke 21:25–36

ADDITIONAL SCRIPTURE READINGS
Psalm 25:1–10; Jeremiah 33:14–16; 1 Thessalonians 3:9–13

---

[25] "There will be signs in the sun, moon and stars. On the earth, nations will be in anguish and perplexity at the roaring and tossing of the sea. [26] People will faint from terror, apprehensive of what is coming on the world, for the heavenly bodies will be shaken. [27] At that time they will see the Son of Man coming in a cloud with power and great glory. [28] When these things begin to take place, stand up and lift up your heads, because your redemption is drawing near." [29] He told them this parable: "Look at the fig tree and all the trees. [30] When they sprout leaves, you can see for yourselves and know that summer is near. [31] Even so, when you see these things happening, you know that the kingdom of God is near."
—Luke 21:25–31

From Anxiety to Anticipation

God loves a good question. If a question is good, God can't help but answer.

One of my favorite songwriters says she was at her piano, frustrated with writer's block, when she just flat-out asked God, "If you could say anything to the world right now, what would it be?"

In that moment, she heard God speak. "Fear not. If I could say it any louder, I would."

I've thought about this story several times since I heard it. It instantly emboldens me to think that God—the only one who actually knows how this whole humanity thing is going to shake out—is standing on a proverbial street corner somewhere, shouting, of all things, "Fear not!" I imagine God holding a bullhorn of absolute peace, asking, "Can anyone hear me? How do I turn this thing up?" That being said, when I turn to Luke 21 and read the entire chapter, which I encourage you to do as well, I admit my emboldened heart grows a bit weak at the knees. This passage should come with a warning label. In just a few verses, Jesus places his finger on the very spot in our hearts where all the anxiety, fear, and chaos live.

Jesus preaches one of his most terrifying sermons in this chapter, interweaving prophecy about the coming destruction of the Jewish temple with prophecy about the end of the world. In these verses, Jesus tackles (exposes?) the low-level anxieties we have on a daily basis: fears about provision, relationships, and future are cranked up to apocalyptic levels.

But in the midst of all this seemingly bad news, Jesus makes two "fear not" statements. Taking it a step further, he then adds that not only should we not be anxious, we should actually be expectant. When you see these things, "stand up and lift up your heads, because your redemption is drawing near" (v. 28). How is it possible to be unafraid under such circumstances? The answer to this question is hidden in the story of the widow and her offering, found at the beginning of Luke 21. Responding to the Father, surrendering all, she gives us a simple picture of the way God moves our hearts from anxiety to anticipation.

"The strange thing is that we are perhaps most afraid of the solution to our anxiety," writes Caroline Coleman in a chapter on her blog that focuses on Luke 21. "We fear giving God everything. We prefer to hold back. The widow who gives all that she has, therefore, is a model for each of us. She is a model for how our peace comes from trusting God completely. The more we give to God, the more peace we will have."

Take a moment to listen. Can you hear it? Inside the sound of your two coins rolling around the bottom of the plate—such a feeble offering—lies a very good question.

"God, will you come through for me again?"

God will.

—**Elizabeth Perry**

Questions for Discussion or Reflection

1. God asks for nothing but that which God has already empowered us to surrender. Take a moment to quiet yourself before the Lord and listen. What is God asking you to release into God's hands?

_____

_____

_____

_____

_____

_____

2. Consider what the songwriter mentioned in this reflection heard God tell her: "Fear not. If I could say it any louder, I would." In what ways does this statement surprise, challenge, or inspire you?

_____

_____

_____

_____

_____

_____

_____

3. In what ways can we live and spread a "fear not" message in the world? What is one thing fear has kept you from doing? Put another way: If fear were not a factor, what is one thing you would do?

_____

_____

_____

_____

_____

_____

_____

4. What was the message of hope for you personally in this reflection?

_____

_____

_____

_____

_____

_____

_____

TODAY'S SCRIPTURE READING
2 Peter 3:1–18

ADDITIONAL SCRIPTURE READINGS
Numbers 17:1–11 and Psalm 90

---

[10] But the day of the Lord will come like a thief. The heavens will disappear with a roar; the elements will be destroyed by fire, and the earth and everything done in it will be laid bare.

[11] Since everything will be destroyed in this way, what kind of people ought you to be? You ought to live holy and godly lives [12] as you look forward to the day of God and speed its coming. That day will bring about the destruction of the heavens by fire, and the elements will melt in the heat. [13] But in keeping with his promise we are looking forward to a new heaven and a new earth, where righteousness dwells.

[14] So then, dear friends, since you are looking forward to this, make every effort to be found spotless, blameless and at peace with him.
—2 Peter 3:10–14

Make Every Effort

Our church is in downtown Lancaster, Pennsylvania, on the corner of Duke and Orange Street, a relatively small church in a small city. Light streams through beautiful, stained-glass windows, and the bell rings in the steeple, calling anyone who would come. A traffic light sits just outside one of the main entrances at the back of the sanctuary, and through those glass doors we often hear motorcycles idling or large semis wheezing to a stop. The courthouse is on the opposite corner, a reminder of the need for judgment in our time.

I find the positioning of this community infrastructure in relation to our church especially poignant during the Advent season.

It's rare for a Sunday to pass without the wail of a siren screaming past. The hospital is only a few blocks away, and even though we live in a small city, it comes with its fair share of accidents, chaos, and misdeeds. Occasionally, after the sirens fade, I wonder: *Where are they going? Who has been hurt? Whose day or week or life has just been drastically altered?*

I sit quietly in church, saying the confession, reciting the creed, taking the sacrament of Communion. Yards away are reminders that our world has more than its fair share of violence, chaos, and destruction. We light the candles in the Advent wreath, but part of me wonders, *Could this ever be enough?*

Likewise, the world described in Peter's second letter is one of chaos and destruction. The writer starts off on a mellow note, exhorting true believers to act in godly ways. But chapter two quickly turns to a review of all that has happened, from false prophets bringing destruction on themselves to sinning angels thrown into hell to await their day of judgment. He ends the second chapter comparing sinners who resume their deviant ways to dogs returning to their own vomit.

Finally, chapter three focuses on the destruction of the planet, in which "the elements will be destroyed by fire" (v. 10).

Well, then.

So how does Peter end his diatribe of destruction? How does he wrap up his letter to those who have lived, or will live, through these apocalyptic times? Does he suggest we scurry around, busying ourselves with the task of survival? Does he implore us to fight back against the very present evil he describes?

Not quite. He has rather different advice.

"And so, dear friends, while you are waiting for these things to happen, make every effort to be found living peaceful lives that are pure and blameless in his sight" (v. 14, NLT).

> *Sometimes, recommitting ourselves to the quiet season of Advent can feel like doing too little in a world that needs so much.*

In other words, even though you have lived through the worst the world has to offer, even though you know the worst is coming, live a life of peace. This is surprising to me—both the advice and its source. This is Peter talking, after all—the same Peter who seemed to want to charge into every situation, acting first and thinking second. Yet now, in the face of all of this, Peter encourages living a peaceful life.

Sometimes, pulling back from the chaos and injustice of the world can feel like an irresponsible act. There are a million and one good causes clamoring for our attention, thousands of good deeds that need doing, and twenty-four hours in every day, each of them calling out to us with some new responsibility, some new requirement. Especially in these days of nonstop media and endless outrage, there is no shortage of voices calling us to urgent, important action.

Do. Do. Do.

Act. Act. Act.

Fight. Fight. Fight.

How can lighting a candle during Advent bring about the change we'd like to see? How can simply waiting for the return of Christ make any difference in a world so far gone? Sometimes, recommitting ourselves to the quiet season of Advent can feel like doing too little in a world that needs so much.

But these weeks of quiet reflection are not wasted.

Today, remember that—in the midst of the chaos, judgment, and destruction—there is another way.

"Make every effort to be found living peaceful lives that are pure and blameless in his sight."

And may this peace infiltrate our over-busy hearts, grounding us, centering us, and enabling us to better reflect the Prince of Peace's love to the aching world around us.

—Shawn Smucker

TODAY'S SCRIPTURE READING
Revelation 22:12–16

ADDITIONAL SCRIPTURE READINGS
2 Samuel 7:18–29 and Psalm 90

---

[12] "Look, I am coming soon! My reward is with me, and I will give to each person according to what they have done. [13] I am the Alpha and the Omega, the First and the Last, the Beginning and the End.

[14] "Blessed are those who wash their robes, that they may have the right to the tree of life and may go through the gates into the city. [15] Outside are the dogs, those who practice magic arts, the sexually immoral, the murderers, the idolaters and everyone who loves and practices falsehood.

[16] "I, Jesus, have sent my angel to give you this testimony for the churches. I am the Root and the Offspring of David, and the bright Morning Star."
—Revelation 22:12–16

Bright Morning Star

For some reason we tend to avoid the Revelation of Jesus to John during Advent. I have always thought that—similar to Matthew and Luke—Revelation has its own Christmas story. In chapter 12, there is a pregnant woman, a child born into a world ruled by political powers who wish to kill him, a powerful angel, and a big mean dragon (kind of like mean old Herod). Maybe we should add a dragon to our family crèche.

The essence of Revelation is gospel—good news in the face of dark realities that confront the people of God living under the rule of Rome. And scattered throughout the Revelation is almost every name for divinity found in Scripture. It is as if John has taken a rake and dragged it though all known Scripture to gather the titles. When you look at the tall pile of names, you begin to see a chronological bent to the titles for Christ. He is the Alpha and the Omega (we would say A to Z), the beginning and the end, the first and the last.

For me, the central title in the book is the declaration that he is the one "who was, and is, and is to come" (4:8). This title is somewhat of a taunt to the Roman emperors who used a similar title, but it is also connected to the story of Moses before the burning bush. When Moses understands that he is to face Pharaoh and demand freedom for the people of God, he asks God, "And whom will I say sent me?" Moses wants a powerful name. He is given this instead: "Tell Pharaoh that that the conjugation of the verb 'to be' has sent you." This is the essence of the name *Yahweh*—the one who was, is, and will be whatever God will be in any given moment in time (see Exodus 3:13–15).

Translated into the Revelation, the one who is currently with them in the present Roman persecution is the one who has always been with them since the beginning of time and also the one who is moving toward them from their future. As this story plays out for twenty-two chapters, time collapses into the eternal, and the Revelation reaches its end with these words: "Look, I am coming soon! My reward is with me, and I will give to each person according to what they have done. I am the Alpha and the Omega, the First and the Last, the Beginning and the End . . . I, Jesus, have sent my angel to give you this testimony for the churches. I am the Root and the Offspring of David, and the bright Morning Star" (Revelation 22:12–13, 16). Once more, we see these chronological bookends of time. Only this time, we get new footnotes with the root of David and the bright morning star.

> *The God who is with us now—the God who has roots going all the way back to David— is the same God who is coming from the future to save us fully and finally.*

Jesus is the one who springs from the tree of David, full of messianic hope but rooted deeply in all the past promises of God. The title "root of David" seems to confirm the was-ness of Jesus, the Alpha/first/beginning.

And "the bright morning star" confirms the will-be of Jesus, the Omega/last/end. This metaphor is rich. In Numbers 22–24, Balak, the son of a threatened Moabite king, hires a holy hit man named Balaam to put a curse on the people of God. Balak has full confidence that whomever Balaam blesses is blessed and whomever Balaam curses is cursed. This holy man is worth his weight in gold. So Balaam receives the offer from Balak—but before signing on the dotted line, he consults God, who tells him that he cannot curse a people who are blessed.

From that point forward, Balaam offers several oracles, but none of them accomplish what Balak wants. Instead, the people of God are blessed repeatedly. In his fourth oracle Balaam declares, "I see him, but not now; I behold him, but not near. A star will come out of Jacob;

a scepter will rise out of Israel" (24:17a). This will not be the last time that the coming ruler from God is viewed as a light in the dark sky. We will hear Isaiah speak of those who walk in darkness seeing a great light, and wise men from the east following a bright star that leads to a future king, and Zechariah singing about the tender mercy of our God dawning from on high to give light to those who sit in darkness.

And here, at the end of the Revelation of Jesus to John, we find the reminder that these words are trustworthy and true. The God who is with us now—the God who has roots going all the way back to David—is the same God who is coming from the future to save us fully and finally. Our future salvation is as sure as the morning star that dawns even as we sleep in the dark. Our God stands in our future, inviting us into tomorrow. Let's go there without fear, with great hope, and with certain joy.

—Dan Boone

TODAY'S SCRIPTURE READING
Luke 11:29–32

ADDITIONAL SCRIPTURE READINGS
Psalm 90 and Isaiah 1:24–31

---

[29] As the crowds increased, Jesus said, "This is a wicked generation. It asks for a sign, but none will be given it except the sign of Jonah. [30] For as Jonah was a sign to the Ninevites, so also will the Son of Man be to this generation. [31] The Queen of the South will rise at the judgment with the people of this generation and condemn them, for she came from the ends of the earth to listen to Solomon's wisdom; and now something greater than Solomon is here. [32] The men of Nineveh will stand up at the judgment with this generation and condemn it, for they repented at the preaching of Jonah; and now something greater than Jonah is here.
—**Luke 11:29–32**

The Sign of Jonah

It is not uncommon to hear Christians speak of signs from God. Indeed, many Christians ask God for signs, hoping to verify God's presence or activity in particular situations. One might ask for assurance from God that a loved one who is ill will be healed, or a confirmation from God that a right decision has been made in a tricky situation. One might ask for an experience from God that will attest to God's nearness, or a blessing from God that will strengthen one's faith. At times, even churches desire signs from God. A spike in attendance or an emotionally charged service might prove, perhaps, that God is working in the church.

In the eleventh chapter of Luke, Jesus offers a surprising assessment of the desire for signs, following an incident where he cast out a demon from and restored the speech of a man who was mute (v. 14). As is often the case in the Gospels, the work of Jesus generates a mixed response: some are in awe at the healing; some accuse him of colluding with Beelzebul (i.e., Satan); and others ask "for a sign from heaven" (v. 16).

After Jesus refutes the claim that he casts out demons by the power of Beelzebul (vv. 17–26), he addresses those who desire a sign from him, unexpectedly delivering a sharp rebuke. "This is a wicked generation. It asks for a sign, but none will be given it except the sign of Jonah. For as Jonah was a sign to the Ninevites, so also will the son of Man be to this generation" (vv. 29–30).

Why does Jesus criticize, in such strong terms, those in the crowd who ask for a sign, referring to them as "wicked"? In the New Testament, a sign (Greek: *semeion*) is simply something that points beyond itself. Up to this point in Luke, Jesus has performed numerous signs: healing the sick and disabled, enabling a great catch of fish, casting out demons, calming the winds and waves, and feeding the five thousand. These various signs all point to the power of God in Jesus. They point to the coming of the kingdom in his person. Luke tells us that even Jesus's disciples performed many signs, for they were given a share in his own power (9:1–2; 10:17–19).

In light of the occurrence of so many signs in Jesus's ministry thus far, the crowd's request for *another* sign suggests that they are simply interested in seeing dramatic displays of divine power, rather than nurturing a sincere desire to believe in and follow Jesus. Luke says they kept asking Jesus for a sign specifically "from heaven" (v. 16), perhaps something akin to the pillar of cloud their ancestors saw (Exodus 13:21). Everything they've seen thus far has not been enough for the crowd; they want a more elaborate, more cosmic sign to dazzle them and satisfy their curiosity.

> *Advent calls us to recognize the time of our visitation from God in the daily rhythm of our lives and in the basic practices of the church.*

Moreover, in desiring a sign from heaven, the crowd overlooks the greater sign that is right in front of them: the person of Jesus. This oversight is the heart of Jesus's rebuke, and the rebuke becomes even more pointed when Jesus refers to Jonah and the people of Nineveh. When Jonah went to Nineveh (a city of gentiles who were known for their great wickedness), he offered no signs other than the sign of his own person and word. That sign was enough, however, to lead the entire city to repentance. Now, a greater sign than Jonah is present among the people of Israel—God himself in the person of Jesus. Even so, the people do not see this sign or accept it. Because they long for a sign *from* God, they miss the ultimate sign *of* God: the person of Jesus. In desiring a sign from heaven, they fail to recognize the visitation of God on earth (Luke 19:44).

Jesus's assessment of the crowd's desire for signs is an important challenge to us this Advent season. We are not entirely unlike the crowd, for there are times when we focus so much on what Jesus can give us that we lose sight of the gift of Jesus himself. There are times when we yearn so much for signs from God that we miss out on God himself, who is faithful to make himself known to us in real but ordinary ways: in the proclamation of the Word, in the bread and cup of the Lord's Supper, in the worship of the church, in the quiet stillness of private prayer, or in our encounters with those on the margins.

St. Augustine wrote in *On the Trinity*, "How great a God is he who gives God!" The ultimate gift—the ultimate sign—is God, who comes to us in the incarnate Christ and the indwelling Spirit.

Rather than seeking signs from God, Advent calls us to recognize the time of our visitation from God in the daily rhythm of our lives and in the basic practices of the church. "And now something greater than Jonah is here," Jesus tells us in Luke 11:32. May we all have eyes to see the sign who is God, present among us through Christ and the Spirit. This sign alone is enough.

—Scott Dermer

TODAY'S SCRIPTURE READING
Malachi 3:5–12

ADDITIONAL SCRIPTURE READINGS
Luke 1:68–79 and Philippians 1:12–18a

---

[7]"Ever since the time of your ancestors you have turned away from my decrees and have not kept them. Return to me, and I will return to you," says the LORD Almighty.

"But you ask, 'How are we to return?'

[8]"Will a mere mortal rob God? Yet you rob me.

"But you ask, 'How are we robbing you?'

"In tithes and offerings. [9]You are under a curse—your whole nation—because you are robbing me. [10]Bring the whole tithe into the storehouse, that there may be food in my house. Test me in this," says the LORD Almighty, "and see if I will not throw open the floodgates of heaven and pour out so much blessing that there will not be room enough to store it. [11]I will prevent pests from devouring your crops, and the vines in your fields will not drop their fruit before it is ripe," says the LORD Almighty. [12]"Then all the nations will call you blessed, for yours will be a delightful land," says the LORD Almighty.
—Malachi 3:7–12

Bring the Whole Tithe

It seems the Christmas season works to bring out the best in people. We feel inspired to put money in the red kettle for the Salvation Army, knowing they will be ministering to people in need. We bake cookies to share with neighbors, family members, and friends as a sign of love and fellowship. Donations to charitable organizations reach their annual peak as people share the spirit of Christmas with others. Volunteers flock to shelters to serve the homeless. Families and churches fill shoeboxes with goodies to send around the world. All of these things are done because there is something about the advent of the Messiah that draws us into his compelling story and life of selfless sacrifice.

The Old Testament repeatedly foreshadows the arrival of the Messiah. We are being pulled toward a future that God has already prepared. The prophetic words point toward a time when the advent of the Messiah will transform the hearts of God's people. The foreshadowing alludes to the Christ who will usher in an era when the great commandment to love God and love others will become our sacrifice of praise.

Jesus's parents were poor and displaced at the time of his birth. Jesus willingly gave up what he was to become what we are and, in doing so, brought healing for all of humanity. The hired worker, the widow, the orphan, and the foreigner are all symbols of ourselves. We are humans in desperate need of a Savior. The advent of the Messiah ushers in a tide change in which these who are on the margins will be swept up in the love of God revealed in the lives of those who are following Jesus. This is the vision of the prophet: an era when God's people would learn to love others more than themselves.

A change of heart results in a change of behavior. The Advent season seems to help us open our eyes to see others around us in a different light. Suddenly we become concerned about the seasonal worker at the store where we are doing our Christmas shopping. Will they receive a decent wage and be able to enjoy the holiday with their loved ones? We take a few moments to linger at the checkout counter and have a little conversation.

We have widows in our midst as well—the friend who has lost a spouse this past year and is experiencing a year of firsts. The first Christmas season without the spouse, and everything about it brings a flood of memories and emotions. Then there is the foreigner who has

> *There is something about the advent of the Messiah that draws us into his compelling story and life of selfless sacrifice.*

moved in just down the street, a person from another land whom we are compelled to love and welcome. Reaching out to the immigrant is a celebration of the advent of the Messiah. Our behavior toward those who are new to our communities is a reflection of our participation in the new kingdom ushered in by Jesus, the baby born in a town far from home.

The prophet could see the dawning of the new kingdom on the horizon and the love of God poured out into others spilling across the land in hues worthy of a masterpiece. That light dawning was just the beginning, a light that was drawing the people back toward their God. They were to be a people who were faithful to participating so fully with God that God's very character would be revealed in and through each and every one of them. Just as Jesus gave himself up for a world full of sinners, so the light dawning would spread love to those on the margins. Love for God would be demonstrated in faithful giving, from a heart overflowing with a spirit of generosity. This was the advent of a time when God's people would love others, the widow, the foreigner, the orphan, and God with their whole being.

As the light of Advent spreads, so does our spirit of generosity. This time it reaches up to the heavens as we participate in God's plan to support the bride of Christ, the church. Tithes and offerings aren't optional but, rather, are sacrificial gifts of love that come from hearts filled with gratitude and generosity. Our tithes and offerings become a symbol of our love for our holy God. The prophet, knowing this, rebukes God's people for refusing to live in the light that is dawning. Instead, they keep all they can for themselves, making excuses about their inability to give to God, and in their greed, they completely miss out on God's own generosity.

In our participation with God's generosity, we receive in return. As the light dawns, let's take upon ourselves the challenge from God. Let's live in a spirit of generosity, giving to God and to others, and see what happens this Advent season. Who knows—we may become participants in a new and glorious masterpiece that is the advent of Christ.

—Carla Sunberg

TODAY'S SCRIPTURE READING
Philippians 1:18b–26

ADDITIONAL SCRIPTURE READINGS
Luke 1:68–79 and Malachi 3:13–18

I will continue to rejoice, [19] for I know that through your prayers and God's provision of the Spirit of Jesus Christ what has happened to me will turn out for my deliverance. [20] I eagerly expect and hope that I will in no way be ashamed, but will have sufficient courage so that now as always Christ will be exalted in my body, whether by life or by death. [21] For to me, to live is Christ and to die is gain. [22] If I am to go on living in the body, this will mean fruitful labor for me. Yet what shall I choose? I do not know! [23] I am torn between the two: I desire to depart and be with Christ, which is better by far; [24] but it is more necessary for you that I remain in the body. [25] Convinced of this, I know that I will remain, and I will continue with all of you for your progress and joy in the faith, [26] so that through my being with you again your boasting in Christ Jesus will abound on account of me.
—**Philippians 1:18b–26**

To Live Is Christ

The Advent season is often overshadowed by the glitter and glory of Christmas hot on its heels. Every store is festooned in bright colors and glitter, and the music is jolly and joy-filled. But, for many of us, these joyous celebrations and bright-colored packages are reminders of what we don't have.

In our own faith community, we have a family with a father who is incarcerated, others who have recently lost family members, and families experiencing financial difficulties. This season, though culturally joyful, can be a time of increased suffering for some. In these moments, it is easy to see where Paul is coming from in Philippians. Torn between wanting to fulfill his earthly obligations to advancing the cause of Christ and wanting to just be done with this world, with the pain, with waking up each morning with the knowledge of torment to come. So many of us can relate to the desire to pull the covers up over our heads and just ask for a redo on the day, the month, the year.

We have all faced suffering in one form or another, and and we have all woken up to days when we would rather hide than face the world. There are circumstances and people we'd rather not see, and the idea of waking up instead to the glory and presence of Jesus is appealing. It would be easy to sink into escapism, to hide away and try to keep oneself as safe as possible from the hardships of the world.

But the message of the incarnation is not one of escapism; it is a message of a God who enters into suffering with us. A God who left the glory of heaven and entered into a time of great suffering among a people who were well acquainted with grief and sorrow. A God who chose to enter into suffering with God's people, in order that they may not suffer alone.

There is hope in that message. We do not need to escape suffering to encounter God because God is already present with us. We do not need to have perfect lives without hardship, anguish, or sorrow because we know that God has already entered into those areas of hardship with us. If nothing else, we live in the knowledge that we do not walk alone.

> **Advent is not about trading in our suffering for jolly songs and bright packages; it's about finding hope in the midst of the pain.**

Advent is not about trading in our suffering for jolly songs and bright packages; it's about finding hope in the midst of the pain. It's about acknowledging that there is a God who hears our cries, who enters into our pain with us, and who ultimately desires to redeem that pain.

This season might be a season of suffering for you—from grief, loss, anxiety, or depression—and it's easy to feel lost in the swirl of red and green. It's easy to begin to think that your feelings don't matter or are overlooked, but the message of this season is that God hears the cries of the brokenhearted, and does something about them. God is not distant. God enters into suffering humanity to walk with us, and God desires to walk with you too. There is hope that your silent cries will not go unanswered and that even this will be redeemed.

This season, whether filled with joy or sorrow, is also a time when we, like Paul, can learn the importance of being the presence of Christ for others. Advent can be a reminder for us to listen to the cries of those who suffer and to come alongside them with our presence. To illustrate to them through our actions that they are not forgotten. To bestow within them hope, even in the midst of suffering. To be the hands and feet of Christ through baked goods and hugs, through warm cups of tea and a smile—but ultimately through our presence that walks in community with those who suffer, offering hope in the midst of pain.

So whether you are filled with joy or anguish today, know that God is not distant. God is listening to you and draws close to you through it all. May you find a hope this season that grows so big that you learn to share that hope with the world through your own presence, as you walk alongside those who need you to be present for them. May we learn not to shy away from pain but to listen to each other's cries and walk alongside one another as we learn to bring hope and light to a world that desperately needs it—this season, and always.

—Robbie Cansler

TODAY'S SCRIPTURE READING
Luke 9:1–6

ADDITIONAL SCRIPTURE READINGS
Malachi 4:1–6 and Luke 1:68–79

---

1 When Jesus had called the Twelve together, he gave them power and authority to drive out all demons and to cure diseases, 2 and he sent them out to proclaim the kingdom of God and to heal the sick. 3 He told them: "Take nothing for the journey—no staff, no bag, no bread, no money, no extra shirt. 4 Whatever house you enter, stay there until you leave that town. 5 If people do not welcome you, leave their town and shake the dust off your feet as a testimony against them." 6 So they set out and went from village to village, proclaiming the good news and healing people everywhere.
—Luke 9:1–6

Proclaiming the Good News

Advent is a season of contradictions. It's a season of strangling darkness and stubborn light. It's a season of despair and a season of trust. It's a season that reminds us of our failures and a season when we celebrate the birth of the only one who can redeem our past.

At its core, Advent is the season of hope: the promised one was born in Bethlehem. Advent is also the tragic story of the death of countless newborns. The soundtrack of Advent is the cries of God's people: "God, save us!" and "God, why have you left us alone?"

Many of us feel the Advent contradiction in a profound way. Wounded parents gather, celebrating the birth of the Messiah in a back-alley manger while their minds wander, worrying about their own firstborn, lost in some unknown back alley, searching for a fix. There are those who sing songs about a newborn babe while silently weeping over the loss of a little one who didn't see their first birthday. Others read this story of an immigrant family fleeing an oppressive regime and find themselves worrying about their own precarious citizenship situations.

Yes, Advent is complicated and can weigh heavily on our hearts. Like those unsuspecting Bethlehem mothers and fathers, how many of us feel like the Christ child came and we're the ones who suffered the fallout? Advent, in its moments of darkness and anticipation, has a way of bringing to the surface years of pain that feels as though it will tear us apart. This leaves us asking a difficult question: How do we hold the tension of this season without finding ourselves torn apart? Advent, in all its painful and hopeful contradictions, teaches us that the only lasting answer is to bind ourselves to hope.

There's *something* about the birth of this light—small and seemingly insignificant—that stands in opposition to the unrelenting darkness all around us that's different, isn't there? For the Jews, it was a light that stood in opposition to the Roman Empire. For us, the light stands in opposition to the dominant voices of our own lives: The voices that accuse. The voices that shame. The voices that remind us of our past. The voices that take away every moment of joy. The voices that assault our hearts. The voices that drive us to self-medicate. The voices that cause us to harm ourselves. The voices that blame, point, and accuse. The voices that tell us we'll never be loved for who we are. The voices that tell us no king would ever allow such a broken jar to be used for such an important purpose.

How dare you hope! the voice says with a sneer. *What right do you have to hope your future will be better than your present?*

Herein lies the good news of Advent. The hope of Advent reminds us the Light was born, and its arrival broke the curse, revealing those voices around us and within us to be liars. The Light has come and revealed this isn't the way it'll always be. The Light has come and declared that darkness has its limit and the kingdom of God exists not for the ones who have it all together but for the ones who are falling apart.

This is good news for all of us because we each carry, deep inside, a storehouse of pain and suffering (both spoken and unspoken). We carry illness. We suffer injustice. We feel sadness, experience depression, weep with loneliness, and scream from anxiety. We have felt the sting of loss and the deaths of friends, family members, and dreams.

There is a great thrill in this invitation to hope, though. Believing, against all odds, that we are the ones—wounded and falling apart though we may be—for whom this baby in Bethlehem was born. In fact, the greatest mystery of Advent is how God uses the apparent contradictions and wounds within us to light the way for others. The thrill of hope is that we're brought to the table, cracks and all, served and poured out for the sake of the gospel, and our stories—full of hurts and imperfections—are the life stuff of the emerging kingdom.

This Advent, as we sit in our seats or stand behind our pulpits, and as our minds race with doubt, pain, regret, and shame, may we remember the thrill of hope: that God has not forgotten us or our loved ones, has not given us up for dead or wiped his hands clean of us. Instead

> *The hope of Advent reminds us that the Light has come and declared that darkness has its limit.*

the Messiah, at his most vulnerable, entered into those back-alley spaces, filling darkness with light and giving hope to the forgotten.

May we surrender to this hope, in all our doubts and imperfections. For it is through the cracks in our hearts that the Light shines most brightly. Thanks be to God.

—Michael Palmer

The Way of
HOPE

Second Sunday of Advent
DECEMBER 9, 2018

Weekly Prayer

My Lord God, I have no idea where I am going.
I do not see the road ahead of me.
I cannot know for certain where it will end.

Nor do I really know myself,
and the fact that I think that I am following your will
does not mean that I am actually doing so.
But I believe that the desire to please you does in fact please
   you.
And I hope I have that desire in all that I am doing.
I hope that I will never do anything apart from that desire.
And I know that if I do this you will lead me by the right road,
though I may know nothing about it.

Therefore will I trust you always,
though I may seem to be lost and in the shadow of death.
I will not fear,
for you are ever with me,
and you will never leave me to face my perils alone.

—Thomas Merton

MEMORY VERSE CHALLENGE

Then John went from place to place on both sides of the Jordan River,
preaching that people should be baptized to show that they had
repented of their sins and turned to God to be forgiven.
—Luke 3:3 (NLT)

Come to the Table

SUNDAY SCRIPTURE READING
Luke 3:1–6

ADDITIONAL SCRIPTURE READINGS
Malachi 3:1–4; Luke 1:68–79; Philippians 1:3–11

---

¹ In the fifteenth year of the reign of Tiberius Caesar—when Pontius Pilate was governor of Judea, Herod tetrarch of Galilee, his brother Philip tetrarch of Iturea and Traconitis, and Lysanias tetrarch of Abilene— ² during the high-priesthood of Annas and Caiaphas, the word of God came to John son of Zechariah in the wilderness. ³ He went into all the country around the Jordan, preaching a baptism of repentance for the forgiveness of sins. ⁴ As it is written in the book of the words of Isaiah the prophet:
"A voice of one calling in the wilderness,
'Prepare the way for the Lord,
make straight paths for him.
⁵ Every valley shall be filled in,
every mountain and hill made low.
The crooked roads shall become straight,
the rough ways smooth.
⁶ And all people will see God's salvation.'"
—Luke 3:1–6

The Way of Holiness

I was several hours into a drive from Illinois to Florida when I realized something wasn't right. My friend and I had typed the words "Daytona Beach" into Google Maps and hit the road, but several hours into our drive, we had yet to see an interstate. Our journey had so far consisted entirely of side streets and country back roads. Exasperated, I pulled over to consult our Google guide.

"Where are you taking us, you fool?" I yelled into my smartphone.

When I examined the route options more closely, my phone seemed to yell back, "You programmed the navigation for bike path, you fool!"

We course corrected, and about a half hour later we found our way to a beautiful, glorious interstate on-ramp. There is something romantic about taking the road less traveled, but for my friend and me that day, our hope lay in the highway.

The prophet Isaiah also found hope in highways. For him, they represented the idea of access—to God's presence, land, and endless blessings. "And a highway will be there; it will be called the Way of Holiness," he declares in chapter 35, verse 8.

The most famous road metaphor Isaiah ever used is probably found in chapter 40: "A voice of one calling: 'In the wilderness prepare the way for the Lord; make straight in the desert a highway for our God. Every valley shall be raised up, every mountain and hill made low; the rough ground shall become level, the rugged places a plain. And the glory of the Lord will be revealed, and all people will see it together'" (vv. 3–5).

Isaiah spoke these words after announcing that, because of Israel's sin, God was going to allow Babylon to overthrow Jerusalem and the people would be exiled from their own nation and sent to live elsewhere. However, he was quick to follow the bad news with the promise in chapter 40 of coming deliverance. And, just as Isaiah foretold, a hundred years later, the Israelites found themselves exiled and held in captivity in a foreign land. Isaiah's blessing, however, also had its full effect. God laid a path for Israel's redemption. God overthrew their enemies. God brought them home.

Turning, then, to Luke 3:1–6, what does it mean when John the Baptist walks onto the scene almost six centuries later, echoing Isaiah's words? In John's day, Israel is neither in exile currently nor going into exile any time soon. Yet, while John's words have geo-political implications—because Jesus is King over real kings and actual kingdoms—this time the message is also much more personal. A Savior is coming who will do more than provide Israel access to their own land: he will provide humankind access to the very heart to God. The Way of Holiness, as it turns out, is a living person.

John preaches repentance. The Greek word for repentance is *metanoia*, which means "to turn around or change directions." And so we repent—but not in a self-involved, legalistic way. We simply take our navigation off the bicycle setting and stop trying to pedal our way to paradise by way of self-righteousness and pride. Instead, we lean into God's presence and begin to feel the wind on our faces as God places us on a beautiful, unobstructed stretch of road that is designed for expedited travel and momentum.

Will the journey be without difficulty? Hardly. But we rejoice because, in repentance, we do not find a way to get to God. In repentance, we find a sign that God has already gotten to us.

God our highway. God our hope. God our way home.

—Elizabeth Perry

Questions for Discussion or Reflection

1. Isaiah knew how important it was to have access to God's blessings. What are some of the promises God has given you?

_____

_____

_____

_____

_____

_____

2. In what ways is it fitting for Jesus to be described as the Way of Holiness?

_____

_____

_____

_____

_____

_____

_____

3. What role has repentance played in your life? Did any of your views on repentance change after reading this piece? If so, which ones?

_____

_____

_____

_____

_____

_____

4. Think about an area in your life where God has challenged you recently. Instead of guilt or shame, how can you receive God's correction as good news?

_____

_____

_____

_____

_____

_____

MONDAY, DECEMBER 10, 2018

TODAY'S SCRIPTURE READING
Isaiah 40:1–11

ADDITIONAL SCRIPTURE READINGS
Psalm 126 and Romans 8:22–25

---

¹ Comfort, comfort my people,
says your God.

⁶ A voice says, "Cry out."
And I said, "What shall I cry?"

"All people are like grass,
and all their faithfulness is like the flowers of the field.
⁷ The grass withers and the flowers fall,
because the breath of the Lᴏʀᴅ blows on them.
Surely the people are grass.
⁸ The grass withers and the flowers fall,
but the word of our God endures forever."
—Isaiah 40:1, 6–8

The Grass Withers

I'm suspicious of the word *balance*. Whenever I'm encouraged, critiqued, or otherwise pressured to find "balance" in my life, I'm reminded that the person using the word gets to define it. In other words, balance seems to be a moving target—a mythical, subjective, nebulous, intangible goal that seems always to elude my grasp.

It's not that I don't believe in imbalance. To be sure, I've experienced terrible imbalance in my life, and the consequences aren't pretty! Tension, frustration, failure: these are a few of the ways to describe the toxic exhaust of an unbalanced life. Unlike an unattainable sense of balance and perfect equilibrium, which seems to be beyond us, imbalance and the effects of imbalance seem to pop up everywhere, and—like so many other things—you know it when you see it.

And sometimes, it looks beautiful. Sometimes imbalance is breathtakingly beautiful. Sometimes, out of whack is exactly what God intends, and sometimes God is most clearly identified in gracious inequity. Now we're moving toward Isaiah 40.

The people of God have made an awful, incalculable, catastrophic mess of things. Though they'd been warned thousands of times, the people ignored the voices of God and God's prophets, choosing instead other gods and empty pursuits and wandering into oncoming traffic in the form of the nations of Assyria and Babylon. And they paid dearly. The devastation was thorough, complete, indescribable. Israel, Judah, and Jerusalem weren't just defeated—they were exploded, blown apart, and the effects could be seen from Jerusalem to Assyria to Babylon and in all the deserted, uninhabitable places in between. Things would never be the same.

And, to make it even more painful, Israel deserved it. They'd worked for it. They'd earned their catastrophe. For generations, the people of God denied their God and refused to live within the parameters of the vision of God, and as a result, they faced the painful yet natural repercussions of their rebellion. Exile. Devastation. Death. Darkness.

Most commentators agree that there are three books in the book of Isaiah: first, second, and third Isaiah. Book one (chapters 1–39) details the anguished conversation between God and the wandering, rebellious people of God. The warnings and predictions are realized, and the world goes dark.

And then there's chapter 40. "Comfort my people, says your God." To a people languishing and wasting away in their well-deserved prisons, to a people who lacked the capacity to dig themselves out, to a people who'd long ago wandered away with no hope of finding their way home, God says, "I'm on my way. Get ready."

Though God knows and remembers the sins and frailty of God's people, though God still knows the pain of their wandering and rebellion, God is gathering for a rescue and recovery effort. God is coming for God's people again (and again and again)—because that's what grace does, that's what grace is, and it's totally and completely and beautifully out of balance.

Balance is not a word that should very often (if ever) describe my relationship with the God of grace and rescue. If we're going to be up front about the relationship between and God and the wandering people of God as portrayed in the biblical narrative, we shouldn't very often (if ever) use the word *balance* because this partnership, this covenant, is definitely way out of whack.

It's not that I'm not involved. It's not that God doesn't ache for you and me (and us) to be responsive to this rescuing God. We understand this to be a responsible grace—one that is never fully appreciated or appropriated until or unless we respond in gratitude, humility, and obedience. But let's not pretend we are equal partners in this covenant. Look no further than the biblical witness found so clearly and beautifully in the book(s) of Isaiah: God has a stubborn energy for relationship with the people of God, even and especially when God's people no longer have the imagination or desire or energy to hold up their end of the bargain. Even so, God is always on the way, to rescue and recover and restore the covenant and the covenant partners.

If today, you understand yourself to be in good or great, deep, committed relationship with the God of the story, please understand that, even now, God is doing more of the heavy lifting than you are. There is a blessed and beautiful imbalance at work, and that is good news. Respond in gratitude to the God who seeks you still.

> *Sometimes, out of whack is exactly what God intends, and sometimes God is most clearly identified in gracious inequity.*

If today, you understand yourself to be distant and removed from God, there is still hope. Even if you have made a habit of chasing other gods and wandering away, there is good news. There is grace. There is beautiful imbalance. There is comfort.

Ours is a faith system built on this imbalance. We know we are saved by grace and not by our own goodness or our ability to rescue ourselves. More importantly, God knows it. God knows that we are like grass, withering and blown from here to there. God knows that relationship with folks like us is going to be a little lopsided. Yet, even then, God shows up.

"Comfort my people, says your God." (And you are one of those people.)

—Jon Middendorf

TODAY'S SCRIPTURE READING
Isaiah 19:18–25

ADDITIONAL SCRIPTURE READINGS
Psalm 126 and 2 Peter 1:2–15

---

¹⁸ In that day five cities in Egypt will speak the language of Canaan and swear allegiance to the LORD Almighty. One of them will be called the City of the Sun.

¹⁹ In that day there will be an altar to the LORD in the heart of Egypt, and a monument to the LORD at its border. ²⁰ It will be a sign and witness to the LORD Almighty in the land of Egypt. When they cry out to the LORD because of their oppressors, he will send them a savior and defender, and he will rescue them. ²¹ So the LORD will make himself known to the Egyptians, and in that day they will acknowledge the LORD. They will worship with sacrifices and grain offerings; they will make vows to the LORD and keep them. ²² The LORD will strike Egypt with a plague; he will strike them and heal them. They will turn to the LORD, and he will respond to their pleas and heal them.

²³ In that day there will be a highway from Egypt to Assyria. The Assyrians will go to Egypt and the Egyptians to Assyria. The Egyptians and Assyrians will worship together. ²⁴ In that day Israel will be the third, along with Egypt and Assyria, a blessing on the earth. ²⁵ The LORD Almighty will bless them, saying, "Blessed be Egypt my people, Assyria my handiwork, and Israel my inheritance."
—Isaiah 19:18–25

In That Day

It must have been fascinating to be a biblical scholar before the canon existed in its current form. One thing that continually surprises and impresses me about the Bible is how often it repeats itself and is consistent with its own message. Certainly there are confusing portions that are *in*consistent with other portions, passages that are real head scratchers when we try to read and apply them with modern-day interpretive lenses, and texts that are truly bizarre.

But that's why I'm always impressed when there's a scriptural echo that resonates as clearly as an old set of church bells. And that's what makes me think it would've been fascinating to be one of those who worked so hard to collect and compile the canon we know today, finding those echoes—some, perhaps, for the first time—and making note of them for future readers like myself to marvel at.

Today's scripture from Isaiah contains such an instance, returning us to Exodus. As I read through the passage, I couldn't help but recall the familiar tale of Israel's escape from slavery. And yet, even as they recall that old story, these verses talk about Egypt differently. In the exodus narrative we know so well, Egypt is the villainous nation to be saved *from*. But in Isaiah's prophecy, Egypt has become the nation that is being saved.

Could Egypt—that place of pagan worship, slavery, and hedonistic excess, that place where God surely never dwelt, that place God cursed with nine kinda-weird plagues and one completely devastating plague—could that same place possibly look the way Isaiah prophetically describes? A place where God is worshiped? Where citizens speak the language of God's people? Where God will save and rescue all who live there, who repent of their sins, who turn their hearts to the Lord? It's almost unthinkable.

God did a new thing when God rescued the Israelites from their slavery and oppression in Egypt. Sometimes it's tempting to imagine the exodus as a display of God's forceful wizardry, but God did not use the plagues on Egypt as a mechanism for *forcing* Pharaoh to release the Israelites from their bondage. If that were the plan, God would've only needed one plague. Instead, God allowed Pharaoh to feel and act the way Pharaoh chose to feel and act. And we see the same thing happening in this passage from Isaiah. The prophecy hints at the possibility that God may do a new thing again, bringing Egypt—the ultimate symbol to the Israelites, at this point in their history, of paganism and oppression and godlessness—into the fold of God's people, not by force, but by offering them the choice to repent and be rescued and redeemed.

> *God's plan all along, from the very beginning, has been to save the world that God created so mindfully and carefully.*

It's important for the Israelites to remember, especially since they seem to forget so often, that they are a chosen people for a purpose. They aren't chosen just because God wants to play favorites and tough cookies for anyone who wasn't born into this particular genetic line. Rather, they are chosen to be a promise people *to* the world. They were blessed that they may bless the world.

God's plan all along, from the very beginning, has been to save the world that God created so mindfully and carefully. Later on, when Jesus comes along and opens up salvation and the kingdom of God to *all people*, that welcome of the gentiles that seems so new and revolutionary is merely a repetition of the ancient plan God has been enacting in installments all along the way (with Jesus in full and present cooperation, based on how we understand John 1:1–5). So the resonance of this prophetic text back to Exodus, back to Egypt, back to memories of radical rescue and redemption—these echoes in Isaiah's prophecy are not a mistake.

In the same way, Psalm 126, one of our ancillary texts for today, points *forward* to restoration of all things and the rescue of all people through the incarnation of Christ. That, too, is intentional. To quote the 1994 *Interpretation* Bible commentary on the book of Psalms, Psalm 126 is wholly about "joy remembered and joy anticipated." And, as we know, so is Advent: the birth of Christ remembered and the return of Christ anticipated. In the end, just about everything biblical that matters—"everything necessary for salvation," as some doctrinal language somewhere puts it—points to the saving work of God through the person of Jesus, regardless of whether we're looking back or looking ahead.

—Audra Spiven

TODAY'S SCRIPTURE READING
Luke 7:18–30

ADDITIONAL SCRIPTURE READINGS
Psalm 126 and Isaiah 35:3–7

---

[24] After John's messengers left, Jesus began to speak to the crowd about John: "What did you go out into the wilderness to see? A reed swayed by the wind? [25] If not, what did you go out to see? A man dressed in fine clothes? No, those who wear expensive clothes and indulge in luxury are in palaces. [26] But what did you go out to see? A prophet? Yes, I tell you, and more than a prophet. [27] This is the one about whom it is written:

"'I will send my messenger ahead of you,

who will prepare your way before you.'

[28] "I tell you, among those born of women there is no one greater than John; yet the one who is least in the kingdom of God is greater than he."
—**Luke 7:24–28**

More Than a Prophet

John the Baptist knew something about hope. Scholars say it is likely that he was associated with a community of Jewish hopefuls who lived far away from the bustling center of Jerusalem. His home was out on the margins, at the edge of the wilderness, where he lived, he baptized, and he hoped.

John's hopes were for the restoration of his people—that God would come and fix what was so deeply broken. That brokenness was on display in the apathetic dismissal of his people's sacred calling. John knew they were summoned to be a holy people, to live so closely to God that holiness would saturate their lives and flow over to the lives of others. But when a crowd of his own people came to him, hoping for a baptismal experience, he quickly brought them to the point: "Produce fruit in keeping with repentance," he told them (Luke 3:8). "Anyone who has two shirts should share with the one who has none, and anyone who has food should do the same" (v. 11).

When Jesus came out to be baptized by John, you can detect a sense of the fulfillment of hope in Luke's account. *This* was going to be the man who fulfilled what John and so many others had been waiting for. This would be the man who helped the people of God fulfill their purpose. The thrill of hope surged.

But after Jesus was baptized and began his ministry, a question about that hope began to arise. Rather that doing what John expected, Jesus began doing things like healing the servant of a gentile soldier (7:1–9). He took his time to help people of little consequence, who would never be able to really do much about making God's people act like God's people (7:11–17). And, rather than moving to purify things like the Sabbath, as John likely hoped, Jesus started questioning its very purpose (6:1–10)!

These peculiar actions led John to begin asking questions. "Are you the one who is to come, or should we expect someone else?" (7:20).

> *When the weary are given hope,*
> *the outsider is welcomed, the sick are*
> *healed, and the powerless loved—*
> *the thrill of hope erupts.*

As John's disciples began to tell him what Jesus was actually doing, the thrill of hope began to fade. Whatever John hoped Jesus was going to do, whatever hopes he had placed in Jesus—he was being let down. So Jesus responded, "Go back and report to John what you have seen and heard: The blind receive sight, the lame walk, those who have leprosy are cleansed, the deaf hear, the dead are raised, and the good news is proclaimed to the poor" (v. 22).

I can identify with John here. If I'm honest, I really want God's people to live more fully into their sacred calling. Sometimes I obsess over it. I desperately want God's people to stop claiming the name if they do nothing with the responsibility of that title. I want Jesus to *fix* whatever may be leading to the disconnect between our calling and our action. And I get frustrated when Jesus doesn't seem to do much about it.

I am deeply hopeful for the church. But when God's people get apathetic—when we become content with going through the motions week after week and Jesus doesn't seem to be intervening—the thrill of hope begins to fade.

And then Jesus's words begin to go to work on me. "Look at what I'm doing," he seems to say. "What were you looking for all this time? I'm bringing a hope you couldn't even see." Maybe I've allowed the hopes I have for Jesus to cloud my vision of what he is actually doing.

What was Jesus doing? He was taking weary, broken, poor, gentile outsiders and offering them a welcome. Yes, there were times he addressed the problems he saw with the insiders, but he didn't obsess over them. He moved on to heal the servant of a political enemy, took the time to help someone who would never be able to begin a great movement. The very things that caused John to wonder if Jesus was going to fulfill his hopes were the hallmarks of the kind of hope Jesus was actually bringing. When the weary are given hope, the outsider is welcomed, the sick are healed, and the powerless are loved—the thrill of hope erupts.

Passages like this one help remind me that my hopes, as decent as they may be, are probably too small for what Jesus is actually doing. And this passage also reminds me that if I load up onto Jesus my own shortsighted hopes for what Jesus will do, the thrill of hope will likely begin to fade. But when I hear Jesus say, "Look at what I'm doing," I can begin to sing a familiar song with a renewed sense of awe: "A thrill of hope, the weary world rejoices!"

—Timothy R. Gaines

TODAY'S SCRIPTURE READING
2 Corinthians 8:1–15

ADDITIONAL SCRIPTURE READINGS
Isaiah 12:2–6 and Amos 6:1–8

---

8 I am not commanding you, but I want to test the sincerity of your love by comparing it with the earnestness of others. 9 For you know the grace of our Lord Jesus Christ, that though he was rich, yet for your sake he became poor, so that you through his poverty might become rich.

10 And here is my judgment about what is best for you in this matter. Last year you were the first not only to give but also to have the desire to do so. 11 Now finish the work, so that your eager willingness to do it may be matched by your completion of it, according to your means. 12 For if the willingness is there, the gift is acceptable according to what one has, not according to what one does not have.

13 Our desire is not that others might be relieved while you are hard pressed, but that there might be equality. 14 At the present time your plenty will supply what they need, so that in turn their plenty will supply what you need. The goal is equality, 15 as it is written: "The one who gathered much did not have too much, and the one who gathered little did not have too little."
—2 Corinthians 8:8–15

The Goal Is Equality

The season of Advent is an opportunity for us to re-center our lives around the person and work of Jesus Christ: Immanuel, God with us, the Word made flesh. As we celebrate the birth of our Savior, we share in the ancient longing for the one who rescues, redeems, and restores us to wholeness and holiness. But Jesus did not only come to save us; he also came to *lead* us. At a time when Christmas has become an exercise in overconsumption and busyness, we look to our King to illuminate the path to a more abundant life marked by mercy, grace, and generosity.

Our relationship with money is a spiritual issue. Depending on who's counting, there are approximately two thousand verses in the Bible pertaining to money and possessions. We expend an enormous amount of time and energy trying to earn money, then figuring out how to spend it, manage it, grow it, and keep it. It's more than a little ironic that our currency is stamped with the words "In God we trust" when our actions suggest otherwise. Yet the Spirit helps us recognize our distorted views and practices surrounding money and material things. In response we cry, "Jesus, lead us! Teach us how to be more humble and faithful stewards of the resources you have entrusted to us. Liberate us from our fear of not having enough, for you are Jehovah-Jireh—the God who provides, a loving Father who loves to give good gifts to his children."

God is love. And love manifests itself through giving. "For God so *loved* the world that he *gave* his one and only Son, that whoever believes in him shall not perish but have eternal life" (John 3:16, emphasis added). The connection is clear: God loves, so God gives. Not only that, but God gives at great personal cost. The apostle Paul writes that, though Christ was rich, "yet for [our] sake he became poor, so that [we] through his poverty might become rich" (2 Corinthians 8:9).

We are used to giving out of our excess. We certainly don't impoverish ourselves in the name of charity. But the Son of God laid aside his glory, emptied himself, and took on the nature of a servant, becoming like us in every way. Jesus experienced hunger and fatigue and temptation. He took up our pain and bore our suffering. He gave up his very life, that we might be reconciled to God and become co-heirs in the kingdom of heaven. Christ became poor that we might become rich.

Hear the voice of our Lord as he beckons us to follow his example: "A new command I give you: Love one another. As I have loved you, so you must love one another" (John 13:34). Love manifests itself through giving. Therefore, give freely and generously, without consideration for your own comfort, even at great personal cost, with the hope that others also might have life, and have it abundantly (see John 10:10). This is love in action.

> *We are used to giving out of our excess. We certainly don't impoverish ourselves in the name of charity. But . . . Christ became poor that we might become rich.*

God imparted this grace of Christlike generosity to the Macedonian believers. Paul holds them up as an example to the church at Corinth, talking about how much they gave out of what they did not have. He then exhorts the Corinthians, "See that you also excel in this grace of giving" (2 Corinthians 8:7).

See that you also excel in this grace of giving. Lead us, Lord Jesus, in this more excellent way. Help us to excel in the grace of giving during this special season of remembrance, "that there might be equality" (v. 13). In a time when millions continue to live in extreme poverty and the gap between the haves and have-nots grows ever wider, radical generosity becomes a subversive act. To give beyond our ability so that others might have enough is a sign of the coming kingdom, in which God promises there will be no more death or mourning or crying or pain, for the old order of things will have passed away (see Revelation 21:4).

Generosity is not only about love; it is also about justice, and the conviction that all people are created in the image of God and are, therefore, entitled to share in the resources required for life and human flourishing. Paul's words are clear and unambiguous: "The goal is equality" (2 Corinthians 8:14). Paul compares the generosity of the Corinthian believers to that of the Macedonians to "test the sincerity of their love" (v. 8). Later, he challenges them to examine themselves to see whether they are in the faith (see 2 Corinthians 13:5).

Would you pass such a test? How well does your attitude toward money and your pattern of giving reflect the Spirit of Christ, who lives in you by faith in the Son of God? How does your life compare to the example of the Macedonians? How might you become poor, that others might become rich? How can you excel in the grace of giving this Advent, to the glory of God, for the good of the world?

—Albert Hung

TODAY'S SCRIPTURE READING
Isaiah 12:2–6

ADDITIONAL SCRIPTURE READINGS
Amos 8:4–12 and 2 Corinthians 9:1–15

2   "Surely God is my salvation;
     I will trust and not be afraid.
     The Lord, the Lord himself, is my strength and my defense;
     he has become my salvation."
3   With joy you will draw water
     from the wells of salvation.

4 In that day you will say:

     "Give praise to the Lord, proclaim his name;
     make known among the nations what he has done,
     and proclaim that his name is exalted.
5   Sing to the Lord, for he has done glorious things;
     let this be known to all the world.
6   Shout aloud and sing for joy, people of Zion,
     for great is the Holy One of Israel among you."
—Isaiah 12:2–6

God Is My Salvation

If I close my eyes, I can still see the face of my two-year-old son sinking beneath the glacial waters. I can still see the fear and confusion in his big eyes as he submerged deeper into the lake. Moments before, he was holding onto the rail, as he was told to do. I was turning around to get him a life jacket, and in that split second, Nate decided to step off the safety of the dock. I dropped to my knees and plunged my hand deep below the surface and grasped his little hand to pull him out. I scooped him up and held his shaking body as he cried into my shoulder.

Nate shook off the harrowing experience quite quickly. After his nap, he was ready to venture back out onto the pier again, and the family was able to enjoy an excursion on the lake as we had originally planned. As for me, not even the distraction of the breathtaking mountains was able to keep me from reflecting on the morning's event.

Life is precious. A brush with death will remind you of that. Something shifts, and we are suddenly made aware of our fragility, and we come to appreciate every breath we take as a gift from God. That day on the pier was a reminder of God's steadfastness.

Isaiah 12 is a beautiful song of prophecy to be sung by the people of Judah. It is a hymn of praise and thanksgiving on the lips of a nation compelled to sing and shout for joy because of God's faithfulness. Out of context, this chapter may seem like God's people simply exalting his name out of a heart of worship. Yes, it would be a heart of worship— but also a heart of a nation undergoing affliction. A great calamity would fall upon Judah: an Assyrian invasion, after which the repercussions of war would leave them feeling hopeless and defeated.

The prophet Isaiah promised them that there would be a day of deliverance. God's hand would take hold of his people and draw them to himself like a parent rescuing a drowning child. Judah would be reminded of the Lord's promise that he would never leave them, even in their suffering. They would learn to trust him and fear no longer. God would be their salvation.

As it is often with Scripture, there is a deeper significance to this passage that ought to disrupt our reality. Isaiah speaks not only of deliverance from an oppressive invasion but also of deliverance from death itself. He foretells the coming of the King. "That day" describes the day when God's master plan will be fulfilled through the death and resurrection of his Son, Jesus Christ. Isaiah prophesied that God would deliver a branch from the root of Jesse: the Messiah who would be a great light for the nations of the world. Wonderful Counselor, Mighty God, Everlasting Father, the Prince of Peace—coming to save us all.

> *Get in touch with your fragility in a way that heightens God's steadfastness in your life.*

Christmas is a time of celebration, but for many people, it can be seasoned with profound pain. The festive occasion can accentuate the heartache of a broken marriage or the stress of financial difficulties or an acute awareness that a loved one is no longer with us. Sometimes we find ourselves drowning in our own misery of a broken past, or in depression. Or maybe we are just plain dissatisfied with life. We've become joyless, tired, and lonely.

Isaiah 12 reminds us that the Lord is among us. The Lord himself is our strength and defense. He is a Lord who does not keep his distance. Rather, the incarnational Christ drew close to us in our world of messiness and brokenness. Through his own suffering, the Lord established peace and righteousness as he grasped each of our hands to pull us out of the pit of sin and despair onto solid ground. He saved us. He is saving us. The Lord is our salvation too.

I invite you to celebrate Advent this year by drawing joyfully from the wells of salvation. If you are in a place of despair and hopelessness, trust that he is already working in your life and that there will be a day when his faithfulness will compel you to sing and shout for joy. Get in touch with your fragility in a way that heightens God's steadfastness in your life. There will be times when we cry into his shoulder, but in him we have the security to venture back onto the pier.

In this place of struggle, victory, and welfare, we celebrate the birthday of our Savior. Indeed, his glorious works are worthy to be proclaimed. May the knowledge and experience that the Holy One of Israel is among us make our hearts swell with abundant joy and thanksgiving.

—Christine Hung

TODAY'S SCRIPTURE READING
Luke 1:57–66

ADDITIONAL SCRIPTURE READINGS
Isaiah 12:2–6 and Amos 9:8–15

---

59 On the eighth day they came to circumcise the child, and they were going to name him after his father Zechariah, 60 but his mother spoke up and said, "No! He is to be called John."

61 They said to her, "There is no one among your relatives who has that name."

62 Then they made signs to his father, to find out what he would like to name the child. 63 He asked for a writing tablet, and to everyone's astonishment he wrote, "His name is John." 64 Immediately his mouth was opened and his tongue set free, and he began to speak, praising God. 65 All the neighbors were filled with awe, and throughout the hill country of Judea people were talking about all these things. 66 Everyone who heard this wondered about it, asking, "What then is this child going to be?" For the Lord's hand was with him.
—**Luke 1:59–66**

The Lord's Hand

The way of hope often means first walking the way of discipline. Just ask Zechariah, the father of John the Baptist. As a dad myself, I can't even imagine not being able to declare the news, "It's a boy!" But that's exactly where this old man finds himself. God has blessed him and Elizabeth not just with a child in their old age, but with a prophet. After four centuries of prophetic silence, Israel's hope to hear a word from the Lord has come to pass! But Zechariah has been struck mute because of his unbelief. Maybe God silenced his servant so that his lack of faith and doubt could not spread. We're not sure. But I can't think of a more exacting discipline for a preacher than not being able to speak for nine months!

And now, his newborn son has finally arrived. Of course, everyone assumes Zechariah will want to endow him with his own name. But Elizabeth confused everyone by announcing that he would be called John. Since nobody in their entire family had ever been named John, nobody could understand why Elizabeth would have suggested something so ludicrous. So, of course, they had to ask Zechariah, who had the final say. For the last nine months, Zechariah's only way to communicate would have been to scratch letters on a parchment or some other surface. And now, as he writes down his son's name, I'm sure he vividly recalls the terrible error of doubting God's Word months before. He is not going to make that mistake again! Imagine him emphatically and deliberately writing each letter: *H-I-S N-A-M-E I-S J-O-H-N!* Instantly Zechariah could speak again, and he began praising God.

This was more than just a seminal moment for this old preacher: it was also a renewed sign of hope for all of Israel. "Everyone who heard this wondered about it, asking, 'What then is this child going to be?' For the Lord's hand was with him" (Luke 1:66). Jews hadn't talked like this for centuries. But suddenly you could hear messianic songs of praise coming from Hebrew homes again. God's season of discipline was ending for Israel, and praise filled their mouths. For nine months Zechariah's

> *We don't usually think of discipline as a gift, but it may be God's greatest blessing for you this Advent and Christmas season.*

silence represented the four centuries of Israel's prophetic silence while God completed his season of loving discipline.

It could be that this Advent you find yourself going through a season of God's discipline in your life. Like Zechariah, it could be God's way of purging unbelief from your heart so you can declare his praise in a greater way. Maybe you have walked away from the God you once loved and he has placed his heavy hand of discipline upon you to spare you from the destruction of your own waywardness. Regardless, "do not despise the Lord's discipline, and do not resent his rebuke, because the Lord disciplines those he loves" (Proverbs 3:11–12; cf. Hebrews 12:5–6).

We don't usually think of discipline as a gift, but it may be God's greatest blessing for you this Advent and Christmas season. So resist the temptation to cut that process short. God determines when the discipline is complete, not us. And he designs it not to destroy us but to heal us and build our faith.

We can all learn a lesson from Zechariah—who, when the Lord's discipline ended, did not have one word of complaint. And when it was his moment to speak again, he uttered words of awe-filled praise that flowed from a humble and grateful heart: "Praise be to the Lord, the God of Israel, because he has come to this people and redeemed them. He has raised up a horn of salvation for us . . . to rescue us from the hand of our enemies, and to enable us to serve him without fear in holiness and righteousness before him all our days" (Luke 1:68–69a, 74–75).

If God has given you a voice this Advent, I challenge you to declare Zechariah's prayer of praise right now. Affirm it in your life. Speak it over each and every member of your family. Remind your friends and associates. Declare it to the world. Jesus is our mighty Savior! He is the way of hope.

—Mark Fuller

The Generosity of
HOPE

Third Sunday of Advent
DECEMBER 16, 2018

Weekly Prayer

Take my life and let it be consecrated, Lord, to thee.
Take my moments and my days—let them flow in ceaseless
   praise.

Take my hands and let them move at the impulse of thy love.
Take my feet and let them be swift and beautiful for thee.

Take my voice and let me sing, always, only for my King.
Take my lips and let them be filled with messages from thee.

Take my silver and my gold—not a mite would I withhold.
Take my intellect and use every power as thou shalt choose.

Take my will and make it thine—it shall be no longer mine.
Take my heart—it is thine own; it shall be thy royal throne.

Take my love—my Lord, I pour at thy feet its treasure store.
Take myself—and I will be ever, only, all for thee.

—Frances R. Havergal

MEMORY VERSE CHALLENGE

The crowds asked, "What should we do?"
John replied, "If you have two shirts, give one to the poor. If you have
food, share it with those who are hungry."
—Luke 3:10–11 (NLT)

Come to the Table

SUNDAY SCRIPTURE READING
Luke 3:7–18

ADDITIONAL SCRIPTURE READINGS
Isaiah 12:2–6; Zephaniah 3:14–20; Philippians 4:4–7

---

¹⁰ "What should we do then?" the crowd asked.

¹¹ John answered, "Anyone who has two shirts should share with the one who has none, and anyone who has food should do the same."

¹² Even tax collectors came to be baptized. "Teacher," they asked, "what should we do?"

¹³ "Don't collect any more than you are required to," he told them.

¹⁴ Then some soldiers asked him, "And what should we do?"

He replied, "Don't extort money and don't accuse people falsely—be content with your pay."
—Luke 3:10–14

Humble Generosity

When I was a little girl, my mother taught my sisters and me the old church song "Humble Yourself in the Sight of the Lord." My sisters and I learned this song at that young age when the brain is tender and like a sponge, so the song embedded itself there in the back of my mind, where it remains to this day. And even now, any time I hear someone say in speeches or toasts that they are humbled, or how humbling it all is, that old song rings out in my head.

One day I was listening to a podcast on which a collection of writers sat at a roundtable and discussed the role of the ancient myths in contemporary literature. The youngest poet at the table, when asked what her generation might offer now in the face of so much global hostility, responded, "Listening a bit more carefully. Humbling yourself—" I stopped and rewound the audio by fifteen seconds. "Humbling yourself." There, in some studio in England where artists and authors discussed myth and matters of state, was "humble yourself." The answer to the question posed by the people.

We have never tired of asking for the answers. Much of the Gospels seem to simply be a record of confused people elbowing each other out of the way and trying to get their questions answered. And in the Gospel of Luke, we read about just such a moment: several people asking several questions for several reasons.

John the Baptist has been at the river baptizing believers and preparing the people for the day when the Messiah will walk among them. Then John calls out a group of observers for their lack of authenticity in their pursuit of righteousness. Taken aback, the people panic a little, and they all demand to know right then what *they* need to do to be in the right. Tax collectors, soldiers, and socialites each ask one after the other, "What should we do?" One after the next. And, though John honors each question and responds to each individual, he is really only giving one answer: "Humble yourself."

Give selflessly. Be generous in your expectations. Be honest in all things. Ultimately, lay down your life for others. Humble yourself as a member of your community. As a neighbor. A friend. A sister. A brother. And as a follower of God Almighty. We are called over and over again in the Scriptures to give ourselves away. If you have two shirts, share with the one who has none. Don't take more than you need. Never exploit others for your own gain. Our lives are not the ultimate story. There is only one Life that is the ultimate story—and he too gave his life away. Jesus Christ—Prophet, Priest, and Son of God—died in a fit of pain for no other reason than for someone other than himself. We are reminded—by the one who made the ultimate sacrifice in the ultimate act of generosity—that our lives are not our own.

Humility in its rawest form becomes the greatest illustration of generosity. Selflessness. Whoever may be posing the question and for whatever reason: philosopher, Pharisee, pastor, or poet. There is an answer to the question of how one might live. Humble yourself in the sight of the Lord. And in the sight of the rest of the world, while you're at it.

—Annie F. Carter

Questions for Discussion or Reflection

1. In what ways does humility lead to generosity?

_____

_____

_____

_____

_____

_____

_____

2. Often we think about generosity in terms of finances, but this reflection also mentions a generosity of expectation. What are other types of generosity? What types of generosity are most difficult for you?

_____

_____

_____

_____

_____

_____

_____

3. The act of humbling ourselves in front of God and others feels so personally costly at times. Why do you think that is?

_____

_____

_____

_____

_____

_____

_____

4. With so many crowds gathered around him, John the Baptist could have become proud, but instead he pointed people to Jesus (see Luke 3:15–17). In what specific ways, circumstances, or relationships do you feel called to point beyond yourself to the person of Christ?

_____

_____

_____

_____

_____

_____

_____

MONDAY, DECEMBER 17, 2018

TODAY'S SCRIPTURE READING
Hebrews 13:7–17

ADDITIONAL SCRIPTURE READING
Numbers 16:1–19 and Isaiah 11:1–9

---

[7] Remember your leaders, who spoke the word of God to you. Consider the outcome of their way of life and imitate their faith. [8] Jesus Christ is the same yesterday and today and forever.

[9] Do not be carried away by all kinds of strange teachings. It is good for our hearts to be strengthened by grace, not by eating ceremonial foods, which is of no benefit to those who do so.
—Hebrews 13:7–9

Do Not Be Carried Away

The night before Jesus died he shared a meal with his closest friends, broke bread, gave it to them, and said, "Do this in remembrance of me."

And they remembered. And we remember. But we live in a world in which the only constant thing is change. Culture shifts so fluidly and ceaselessly that it often goes unnoticed. This change has certainly left a mark on our memories.

Our memories are contained in our texting histories and social media posts. We are so afraid that if we don't digitally record an event or a moment, we won't remember it. Ironically, those same devices storing our memories are simultaneously stealing them by stealing our awareness away from so many moments that might have been worth remembering if only we'd been paying attention.

But Jesus Christ is the same yesterday, today, and forever. In the midst of a changing world stands the constancy of Christ. Do you ever worry that—in the midst of such change—we'll lose sight of the Jesus who is the same yesterday, today, and forever? After all, as the hymn reminds us, I know that I certainly am "prone to wander Lord, I feel it, prone to leave the God I love." How do Christ followers cling to eternal constancy when we are living "outside the gate," as Hebrews puts it, in a world of rapid new developments and constant change?

Perhaps we are not the first people to live in a time of fluid cultural change. The author of Hebrews warns the followers of Christ not to be carried away by strange teachings. In order to remain steadfast in Christ in the face of these strange teachings, the people of God are to remember their teachers, consider their lives, and imitate their faith. *Remember. Consider. Imitate.*

We remember those who spoke the Word of God to us. We remember them, their whole being, their personality, their care for us, their flaws, their stories. And, in so doing, we place the faith they spoke to us in the context of the work of God in their lives. The Word of God is more than a list of beliefs or statement of doctrine. The Word of God is alive—like a baby crying in a manger. The Word of God meets us in real life just as it did for the teachers we remember.

> **We know Jesus today because of the faith of so many saints who gave their lives so we could remember.**

As you remember those teachers, don't only think about the words they spoke, but consider the outcome of their lives. I wonder if the disciples considered what the outcome of their lives might be after sharing in the Last Supper. Peter surely considered the outcome of Jesus's life when he denied having known Jesus. He briefly bent under the weight of that consideration. Following Jesus is not to be taken up lightly. For the readers of Hebrews, at least some of these leaders they are stirred to remember surely would have been counted among the martyrs described in Hebrews 11:36–38. Consider the outcome of their faithfulness. Feel the weight of their stories resting on your own life.

After remembering and considering, imitate. The word *imitation* makes me think of a cheap, knock-off product. When viewed that way, no one wants their life to be an imitation. As Hebrews 11 recounts the stories of the faithful teachers and witnesses, they are described as the ones "of whom the world was not worthy." We are being asked to imitate those who followed Christ at a great cost. This form of imitation is anything but cheap. There are plenty of cheap imitations out there. Don't be fooled. Imitate saints. Imitate the lives of those who gave everything. Imitate the people who must never be forgotten. Imitate the ones who looked so much like Jesus that they startled the world.

In a world of constant change, we are prone to wander. That is why every year during Advent we get ready to receive Jesus all over again. We remember, consider, and imitate the Christmas story. We dress our children up as donkeys and sheep, we sing carols that would otherwise be out of date, we put up lights, and we recite the stories of the shepherds, the wise men, the angels, the mother, and the father who all came to welcome the baby.

And we remember. But it must be more than another smiling family photo for your InstaStory. It must be more than a few pictures and posts that will be thrown into the TimeHop until next year. Don't forget: Jesus is the same yesterday, today, and forever. We know him today because of the faith of so many saints who gave their lives so we could remember.

May God the Holy Spirit give you an awareness of the ordinary saints in our midst. May you have the patience to put down your distractions and consider the outcome of their lives pursuing Christ. And as you imitate their faith, may God the Father of our Lord Jesus Christ bind your wandering hearts.

This Advent season, don't miss a moment that is worth remembering.

—**Shawna Songer Gaines**

TODAY'S SCRIPTURE READING
Isaiah 11:1–9

ADDITIONAL SCRIPTURE READING
Numbers 16:20–35 and Acts 28:23–31

---

1. A shoot will come up from the stump of Jesse;
   from his roots a Branch will bear fruit.
2. The Spirit of the Lord will rest on him—
   the Spirit of wisdom and of understanding,
   the Spirit of counsel and of might,
   the Spirit of the knowledge and fear of the Lord—
3. and he will delight in the fear of the Lord.

   He will not judge by what he sees with his eyes,
   or decide by what he hears with his ears;
4. but with righteousness he will judge the needy,
   with justice he will give decisions for the poor of the earth.
   He will strike the earth with the rod of his mouth;
   with the breath of his lips he will slay the wicked.
5. Righteousness will be his belt
   and faithfulness the sash around his waist.

—Isaiah 11:1–5

From the Stump of Jesse

I grew up in western Oregon, which, among other things, is logging country. Most people who live there are involved in the wood products industry in some way. Many in my family are lumber workers and loggers of one stripe or another. A great childhood experience was going up into the woods to watch a logging operation. The precision of the people working with huge chainsaws was amazing. They could drop a 100-foot Douglas fir exactly on target. The other impressive experience as we stood on the mountain ridge was taking in a panorama of the Willamette Valley. The scenery was breathtaking.

A view that was not beautiful, however, was to oversee a clear cut. That's when they log off an entire section of the mountain, leaving nothing behind. Before they replant it, it's a picture of devastation. Tree stumps stretch out before you like pieces on a huge checkerboard. Almost nothing is left of the thick underbrush. This is the kind of picture that Isaiah has In hls mind as we come to chapter 11. Throughout this text, Isaiah announces the coming judgment of God upon Israel. Sometimes the image of this judgment suggests a clear-cut forest. The strong nations of Assyria and Babylon are the wielders of the ax that will cut down the trees of Israel, leaving only desolation behind.

It reminds us of the Gospel lesson in which John the Baptist speaks of the coming of God as an ax "already at the root of the tree" of the house of Israel. "And every tree that does not produce good fruit will be cut down and thrown into the fire" (Matthew 3:10). As Isaiah sees it, this is the condition in which Israel and their neighbors find themselves. It looks completely hopeless. It looks likes there is no way in the world anything could ever be alive there again.

But wait! What's that? Right there in the middle of the field of stumps. It's a little shoot, just an insignificant, little green shoot, but it shines in the middle of the clear-cut field. And suddenly, even though the destruction of the great forest seems total and complete, there is a ray of hope that maybe this forest can live again. This is the hopeful word with which Isaiah opens chapter 11. Against the backdrop of hopeless destruction, Isaiah believes, "A shoot will come up from the stump of Jesse." It is a shoot that will one day give rise to a branch that will again bear wonderful fruit.

Isaiah is offering Israel hope for the future. He is saying that, even as Israel lies destroyed in the wake of God's judgment, God will not leave them in their sin and rebellion. Even at the point when all looks hopeless, God will provide a new hope. It may look rather insignificant at first. Many will miss it altogether, for this new sprig of hope for Israel will come from a most unlikely place. It will come from the stump of Jesse—the least of all the tribes of Israel.

Isaiah is saying that the new hope for Israel will come from the line of David. Remember the story of David's selection as the king of Israel? He was the youngest and smallest son of an insignificant family of the least tribe of Israel. Yet God raised him up and breathed new life into the nation through him. Isaiah is saying that a new day will come when the judgment of God will fall again and all will look lost. But in that moment, our gracious God will provide a little shoot that, one day, will be the salvation of the people.

I don't know how much Isaiah understood about all that he preached, but the church could hear in his words a description of Jesus of Nazareth. By the time Jesus was born, God had been pursuing God's people through a called-out people for centuries. Yet the history of Israel continued to be a sad tale of rebellion and judgment, destruction and restoration. The condition of humankind was like a clear-cut forest. Not much hope of life.

But wait, what's that? There, in a stable in Bethlehem, there's a shoot from the stump of Jesse. There is a ray of hope. It seems so insignificant that most don't notice, but this little shoot will become a branch that will bear great fruit.

This is the call of Advent preparation. We wait in hope in the midst of the destroyed forest and look for the new shoot to pop up. And it comes. It always comes if you have eyes to see. Jesus is the shoot from the stump of Jesse that has come to give us life and peace. In him we have redemption. In him we can find forgiveness and cleansing. Jesus is our hope. And now the risen Christ is at work in this world and in our lives to bring hope to places of destruction.

> *It seems so insignificant that most don't notice, but this little shoot will become a branch that will bear great fruit.*

Perhaps all you can see right now is a destroyed forest. The desolation might be your marriage, or your family, or a child who has turned away from you and broken your heart. Perhaps your health is broken, or a career crashed and burned. You had such hopes, such dreams, yet they stretch out before you now like a burned-out forest.

But wait, what's that? There, coming up through the mud and ashes, a little shoot. There is a ray of hope and a sign that God is bringing life where we would only expect death. It is Jesus, who is making all things new.

—Jeren Rowell

TODAY'S SCRIPTURE READING
Luke 7:31–35

ADDITIONAL SCRIPTURE READINGS
Isaiah 11:1–9 and Micah 4:8–13

³³ "For John the Baptist came neither eating bread nor drinking wine, and you say, 'He has a demon.' ³⁴ The Son of Man came eating and drinking, and you say, 'Here is a glutton and a drunkard, a friend of tax collectors and sinners.' ³⁵ But wisdom is proved right by all her children."
—Luke 7:33–35

By All Her Children

I have a friend who is the funniest person I know. There is only one problem. He doesn't know when *not* to be funny. That internal filter that most people have that helps them to know when it's time to be serious is broken in my friend (if it ever existed).

In Luke's Gospel, although John the Baptist and Jesus are relationally and missionally connected, they are representatives of different eras in the drama of salvation.

John is the prophetic son of a priestly father and a barren mother. He carries the mantle of Elijah and fulfills the expectations of Malachi. Every aspect of his life and story resonates with images from the Old Testament. He is the renewed voice of Isaiah crying in the wilderness, "Prepare the way for the LORD." Not just his message, but also his whole persona invites God's people to know divine judgment, to turn in repentance, and to be ready for newness. In his call to break from the past and its brokenness, he comes fasting and inviting others to back away from tables of plenty and seats of power. This oddness—this otherness—brings ridicule from the religious. He is crazy. He is a misfit. Some say he may even be filled with a demon.

Comparatively, Jesus is the incarnate Son of the heavenly Father and a virgin mother. Although deeply connected to all that God has done in Israel, his life and ministry usher in an entirely new creation. The way has been prepared, and now the glory of the Lord is made known as the blind see, the mute speak, the deaf hear, and the lame dance. Not just his message, but also his whole persona invites all people to know God's grace, to be embraced by divine love, and to enter into a new birth. In his invitation to put to death the old and enter God's kingdom, he feeds multitudes, brings new wine to weddings, and is always ready for a feast. This newness—this turning upside down of the world—also invites ridicule from the religious. He is a rebel. He is a glutton and a drunkard. Some say he is a friend of tax collectors and sinners!

The tragedy in the text for today is the inability of the Pharisees and teachers of the law to properly discern John's call to repentance or hear Christ's invitation to newness. John and Jesus embody different divine times, and unfortunately, the religious miss them both.

I don't know why the religious leaders can't discern the redemptive movement of God in time. I wish I could find the key problem. It would be wonderful if the all-too-common human failure to detect the divine presence could be narrowed down to three points. My guess is that their failure, like ours, is due to some combination of narcissism, false expectations, idolatry, worldliness, spiritual blindness, and self-centeredness in all its various and ugly forms. We are so practiced in observing, honoring, and being entertained by the ways of the principalities and powers that it is hard to see all the ways they form us and even harder to notice the kingdom of God when it comes.

> *Advent reminds us that we are still a people caught between times. We fast because there is still so much darkness to be overcome.*

Our ancestors in faith try to help us discern the rhythms of the kingdom through seasons of feasting and fasting. Advent is mostly fasting. Christmas is mostly feasting. Lent is a fast. Easter is a feast. These patterns, these moments, these movements away from the table and back toward it are attempts to teach us how to discern the need for repentance and to recognize the in-breaking of newness.

Advent reminds us that we are still a people caught between times. We fast because there is still so much darkness to be overcome. We fast because there are too many of our brothers and sisters who are hungry—not by choice but because of oppression. We fast because we are desperate for the way to be made for Christ to come quickly and make all things new.

But we also feast because there is new creation emerging in our midst. We feast because, in the power of the resurrection, sin and death have lost their sting. We feast because we are not simply waiting for Christ's return but are already experiencing him when two or three are gathered together in his name.

This discernment, this ability to know the time, is what the writer of Ecclesiastes lauds as wisdom. And, as Jesus proclaims, "wisdom is vindicated by all her children" (Luke 7:35, NRSV).

—T. Scott Daniels

THURSDAY, DECEMBER 20, 2018

TODAY'S SCRIPTURE READING
Hebrews 10:10–18

ADDITIONAL SCRIPTURE READINGS
Psalm 80:1–7 and Jeremiah 31:31–34

---

[10] And by that will, we have been made holy through the sacrifice of the body of Jesus Christ once for all.

[11] Day after day every priest stands and performs his religious duties; again and again he offers the same sacrifices, which can never take away sins. [12] But when this priest had offered for all time one sacrifice for sins, he sat down at the right hand of God, [13] and since that time he waits for his enemies to be made his footstool. [14] For by one sacrifice he has made perfect forever those who are being made holy.
—Hebrews 10:10–14

We Have Been Made Holy

In pulling out the Christmas decorations, I've moved all of our usual household decor to my bedroom, where it sits on my dresser as a hodgepodge of clutter. Candles, picture frames, souvenirs made of pottery and glass art from various travels. Things that all look right and good when in their place are reduced to what looks like a confused yard sale spread. My dresser itself is a tired piece of furniture with drawers open, clothes spilling out to the floor. Daily, I push the piles back in and close the drawers as best I can, though I know that, somehow, I will do the same tomorrow.

While my youngest daughter helps me crack eggs for a batch of cookies, I notice that she desperately needs to trim her nails. But, she tells me, she likes the way they scratch an itch. Still, where she sees function, I only see the dirt caked underneath, and I insist she trim and wash. When she finally concedes, she reminds me that they're just gonna grow back.

My son splashes the last of our milk all over the kitchen counter while overflowing his cereal bowl—a near daily routine that I typically get to discover and clean while refilling my coffee mug. I add milk to the grocery list. And I sigh.

It's December. It's Christmas and Advent, and I want nothing more than to be filled with the joy of the season rather than the bedraggled exhaustion of these mundane, completely ordinary but entirely overwhelming rhythms and routines of life. Of making my house clean, of keeping my children healthy and fed and in some semblance of order. The endless cycle of making things good enough, of making things right. But then how perfect, in this season, to ponder these routines of keeping things clean and making things right. It's the time when we reflect on the righteousness that was gifted to us, once and for all, in the gentle and mighty gift of a newborn, a Savior.

Accepting that I'm enough, as I am, and that the promise of salvation isn't something I can earn, has always been hard for me. I remember kneeling on the kitchen floor of my childhood home as a girl, nose to the bristle of the muddled brown-and-army-green indoor-outdoor carpet, hands folded above my head, as I prayed the prayer to accept the love and forgiveness of Jesus Christ. I thought of my sins, the times I'd lied to my parents, the sneaking of chocolate chips from the cabinet, the exploring too far into the forest across the street, the places I wasn't supposed to go. And I remember drawing myself back upright, still on my knees, after the "Amen"—and feeling that nothing had changed. Even as a little girl, I knew I would fall short again, that I would need that grace more and more.

> *Grace is, especially, for those who will need it again and again.*

And so, for years, I'd pray the same prayer again and again. *Lord, I love you, and I'm sorry for my sins. Please come into my heart and make it new.* As though I wasn't ever enough for the grace I so desperately craved. My repeated praying of the same prayer wasn't asking for forgiveness at all but was me promising to somehow do better from then on out.

But salvation isn't repetition. It isn't rote and ritual. It isn't for those who try just a *little* harder or have the purest of hearts. It's both simple and complex, and it's for the messy and the cluttered and the utterly flawed just as much as it is for the clean and the put-together. Grace is, especially, for those who will need it again and again.

The gift of salvation has never come by my own doing. It has come not by doing but by accepting and receiving beyond measure. And the promise of salvation is just that—a promise—to us. It's not a wishy-washy, *well, we'll see how you do* type of pseudo-commitment from

God. Rather, it's the gift of a newborn child who became a man who gave all—because we cannot.

My children decorated our tree all by themselves. In the midafternoon sunlight, I stand in the doorway and notice just how dull it looks without the twinkling lights. It's haphazardly trimmed. Too many ornaments are clustered together, clearly the branches my youngest could reach the most easily. A silvery-red strip of bacon ornament is the one most prominently displayed, front and center, even though I would prefer it more tucked away into the evergreen fir. But, this year, I let it be.

Grace is for the child who is asking for forgiveness on a kitchen floor, and it's for the mother who is finally putting down her dish towel and letting the crumbs be. It's for every ugly bit we would rather tuck away. Grace perfects the imperfect because the sacrifice of Jesus was "once for all." And that is the hopeful promise that Advent carries.

—Melanie Haney

TODAY'S SCRIPTURE READING
Hebrews 10:32–39

ADDITIONAL SCRIPTURE READING
Psalm 80:1–7 and Isaiah 42:10–18

---

[32] Remember those earlier days after you had received the light, when you endured in a great conflict full of suffering. [33] Sometimes you were publicly exposed to insult and persecution; at other times you stood side by side with those who were so treated. [34] You suffered along with those in prison and joyfully accepted the confiscation of your property, because you knew that you yourselves had better and lasting possessions. [35] So do not throw away your confidence; it will be richly rewarded.

[36] You need to persevere so that when you have done the will of God, you will receive what he has promised.

[39] But we do not belong to those who shrink back and are destroyed, but to those who have faith and are saved.
—Hebrews 10:32–36, 39

Those Who Have Faith

A number of years ago a new movie theater was built in my neighboring city. The outside looked like a futuristic lair for Lex Luthor. Inside, in the middle of the main traffic area, was a large island that hosted numerous counters for quick ticket and concession lines. They had bottomless popcorn and free refills from space-age soda machines. Perhaps most impressive, and most talked about, was that this new theater boasted memory foam seats. *These chairs will remember you,* they seemed to say. *Think of how comfortable you were for* Star Wars. *When you come back for* Jurassic Park *it will be like you never left! We're not just a movie theater. We're your new home.*

I'll admit, the setup was pretty cool in the beginning. But now, a decade or so later, I choose to go to other theaters in town because those same seats that held such promise have become unbearably rigid and uncomfortable. The thing with memory foam—just like our own memories—is that it can begin to fade and wear out over time. When not properly taken care of, the material can harden. It "forgets" how to be comfortable and how to function as it was designed. The new theater didn't maintain and update their seats so the purpose of those seats became lost.

So, too, are we called to maintain our design and purpose in Christ through remembering—not only for our own sakes but for our neighbor, for the orphan, for the widow, the stranger, the hungry, the naked, the thirsty, and whoever else we come across on life's journey. We are called to remember God's goodness through the good times and bad, until the kingdom comes in all its fullness.

Memory is a powerful faculty in our lives. It can evoke a wide range of emotions: peace, joy, pain, love, and the list goes on. It also provides us with wisdom and discernment. The author of Hebrews encourages his audience to recall how they previously endured in times of trouble. "You have worked through difficult times with boldness and grace," he says. "Remember! God was with you then. God is surely with you now."

This is our Advent refrain as well. Immanuel. God with us then. God with us now.

We are called to remember
God's goodness through the good times
and bad, until the kingdom comes
in all its fullness.

And so, in this season in particular, we remember. We remember how it feels to *wait* for a promised Savior. And we remember our joy when the promise is delivered. Yet Advent isn't merely about looking back. It's also about pressing forward. Our knowledge of the past, after all, shapes both our present and our future. To remember Christ's birth is to live today with anticipation for his coming again. Looking back at how Jesus came, and God's faithfulness to restore and redeem, we can join him in the work of preparing the way for his return.

As partners in the creative and redemptive process, we are to both remember and anticipate. That is the blessed tension we find ourselves in every day. May we recall how God has worked and moved, may we cherish and be inspired by his ways, as well as anticipate how God will continue to work in the days to come. May we make future kingdom realities alive today by how we live. And may we remember our design and steward our vocation.

Recall, my friends. Recall that we are so loved that we ought to go and do likewise and that, always, until the very end of the age, he is Immanuel—God with us.

—**Joshua Kennedy**

TODAY'S SCRIPTURE READING
Isaiah 66:7–11

ADDITIONAL SCRIPTURE READINGS
Psalm 80:1–7 and Luke 13:31–35

---

⁹   Do I bring to the moment of birth
and not give delivery?" says the LORD.
"Do I close up the womb
when I bring to delivery?" says your God.
¹⁰   "Rejoice with Jerusalem and be glad for her,
all you who love her;
rejoice greatly with her,
all you who mourn over her.
¹¹   For you will nurse and be satisfied
at her comforting breasts;
you will drink deeply
and delight in her overflowing abundance."
—Isaiah 66:9–11

You Will Drink Deeply

I can still remember my mother running at a full sprint beside me as we took the training wheels off for the first time, her hand ready to grab me the moment it looked as though I might be going down. I remember yelling her name in panic and how she scaled that pine tree when I had climbed too high and was paralyzed with fear near the top, afraid to make my way down. She told me to trust her as she grabbed onto my shoe, slowly lowering my foot down to the next branch and ultimately guiding me back down to the ground. And then, of course, I remember many of the more simple and mundane things that mothers do with their sons, like going grocery shopping, raking leaves, going to the movies, and hundreds of other little memories that you don't think much of at the time.

My mother has been living with multiple sclerosis for just shy of twenty years now. For her there is no more running. No more climbing. Trips to the grocery store require a motorized cart. No more raking leaves. And, while my mother could still go and see a movie if she wanted to, it's no longer worth the effort and energy it would demand of her. Being able to walk and move about freely is a distant memory.

"Jase, there are days when I am about ready to give up. I've fought pretty hard, but still, there are days when I think I am done." Her honesty when she said this to me caught me off guard. "I'm tired of the severe back pain because I can't stand up straight anymore. I'm tired of the daily leg cramps. I'm tired of not being able to sleep through the night without having to make multiple trips to the bathroom. I'm just tired of always being tired."

I can't help but wonder if this is the type of discouragement the Israelites had come to know toward the end of the book of Isaiah. The life and the freedom they once enjoyed had become little more than a distant memory. They had been cut off from their land. They felt cut off from God. Weariness, oppression, humiliation, defeat, and a loss

> ## *May we find comfort in the God who tells us that one day the darkness will give way to light.*

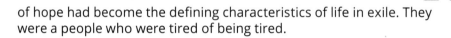

of hope had become the defining characteristics of life in exile. They were a people who were tired of being tired.

And yet, when we read some of the last words from the book of Isaiah, we find God speaking words of maternal hope and comfort: "'Do I bring to the moment of birth and not give delivery?' says the Lord. 'Do I close up the womb when I bring to delivery?' says your God. 'Rejoice with Jerusalem and be glad for her, all you who love her; rejoice greatly with her, all you who mourn over her. For you will nurse and be satisfied at her comforting breasts; you will drink deeply and delight in her overflowing abundance.'" God is telling the Israelites that one day all things will be made new and that their hopelessness, discouragement, and weariness will turn to joy. God has not forgotten them.

Chances are that at some point, each and every single one of us will find ourselves asking the question, *Is this season of my life ever going to pass? Will I be able to make it through this? Will I ever be able to experience the joy and the life I once knew?* Perhaps it's the unexpected and unwelcome diagnosis. Maybe it's the news that in two weeks you will be unemployed with no idea how the bills are going to be paid. Perhaps it's dealing with the harsh realization that it's time to let go of dreams and hopes you've always had. In the midst of these seasons, may we find comfort in the God who tells us that one day the darkness will give way to light. May we find assurance in the God who tells us that things like unemployment, shattered dreams, depression, multiple sclerosis, and even death will never have the final word for those whose hope is in the Lord. Lastly, in the midst of it all, may we give thanks and praise to the God who never leaves nor forsakes his children.

—Jason McPherson

The Promise of
HOPE

Fourth Sunday of Advent
DECEMBER 23, 2018

Weekly Prayer

O holy night! The stars are brightly shining;
It is the night of the dear Savior's birth.
Long lay the world in sin and error pining,
Til he appeared and the soul felt its worth.
A thrill of hope! The weary world rejoices,
For yonder breaks a new and glorious morn!
Fall on your knees!
O hear the angel voices!
O night divine!
O night, when Christ was born!
O night divine! O night, O night divine!

—John S. Dwight

MEMORY VERSE CHALLENGE

You are blessed because you believed that the Lord would do what he said.
—Luke 1:45 (NLT)

Come to the Table

ADDITIONAL SCRIPTURE READING
Psalm 80:1–7; Micah 5:2–5a; Hebrews 10:5–10

[39] At that time Mary got ready and hurried to a town in the hill country of Judea, [40] where she entered Zechariah's home and greeted Elizabeth. [41] When Elizabeth heard Mary's greeting, the baby leaped in her womb, and Elizabeth was filled with the Holy Spirit. [42] In a loud voice she exclaimed: "Blessed are you among women, and blessed is the child you will bear! [43] But why am I so favored, that the mother of my Lord should come to me? [44] As soon as the sound of your greeting reached my ears, the baby in my womb leaped for joy. [45] Blessed is she who has believed that the Lord would fulfill his promises to her!"
—Luke 1:39–45

As Promised

Promises are not made lightly in the Scriptures. When the Lord speaks, it's with authority. And when God's people prophesy, they do the same. It would seem that promises and prophecies are a cornerstone of Christ's language of love. The Scriptures are peppered with them: God will fight for us. God will give us strength. God goes before us and is with us. These are not stories or suggestions. They are guarantees and, thereby, promises to lean on.

The very nature of Advent is an expectant waiting for the fulfillment of a promise that was made. We were promised that Jesus would be born. Promised that he would die. And promised that he would rise again. And in each of those truths, all people then and now were being promised a life worth hoping in. We are not only assured of Christ's life as our Redeemer, but we are also assured of our own lives as precious gifts to be celebrated and cared for each day. We are bodies and souls made whole by the existence of Jesus Christ. Christ's mother, Mary, was one of the first to be promised that such a thing would be true, and she remains a beautiful example of why promises are so full of hope. Life is long and often hard. But even in the moments when we may feel that there is no hope, we can know that there are always promises. And no promise made by God Almighty is left unfulfilled.

In the Gospel of Luke, we see an intimate illustration of Mary's faith in God's promises. A pregnant Mary visited Elizabeth, who was also expecting a child, and when they met, Elizabeth exclaimed that the child within her leapt with joy! She told Mary right then and there that the child Mary was carrying was the Lord (1:43–44). Christ's coming had been foretold for ages, and an entire people had spent their lives hoping for the day when their deliverer would arrive. Elizabeth recognized in that moment that the day had come and that her waiting had not been in vain—and she recognized it despite not being able to *see* it. There is a remarkable lesson in Elizabeth's confidence. Her years of hope and faith brought her to the very presence of the Christ child, and she celebrated it without hesitation.

In the same way that Elizabeth was willing to believe and accept the promises made to her about the future, Mary responded by rejoicing and believing what Elizabeth trusted to be true. Christ was to come. Mary had been told many overwhelming things about what was ahead for her. But in the moment that those foretellings were affirmed in her, she did not resort to questions and concerns as we so often do when what's ahead looks bigger than we are by far. Instead, she rejoiced in what she could see had been a promise of hope from the very beginning. *I have been seen. I have been fed. I have been shown great mercy. Just as he promised.*

—Annie F. Carter

Questions for Discussion or Reflection

1. Just like the promise of a Messiah, the fulfillment of promises in our own lives can require a long period of waiting. Why do you think this is so?

_____

_____

_____

_____

_____

_____

2. Mary's circumstances required her to trust in God beyond what she could see or understand. What is a season or circumstance during which you've had to rely more fully on God?

_____

_____

_____

_____

_____

_____

3. One way to magnify the Lord like Mary is just to thank him for his activity in your life and in the world. Take a moment to write down specific praises of thanks.

_____

_____

_____

_____

_____

_____

4. It's clear from Mary's worship that she understands her pregnancy is about something greater than herself. In what ways might God be blessing you for the sake of the kingdom?

_____

_____

_____

_____

_____

_____

_____

MONDAY, DECEMBER 24, 2018

TODAY'S SCRIPTURE READING
Titus 2:11–14

ADDITIONAL SCRIPTURE READINGS
Psalm 96; Isaiah 9:2–7; Luke 2:1–20

---

[11] For the grace of God has appeared that offers salvation to all people. [12] It teaches us to say "No" to ungodliness and worldly passions, and to live self-controlled, upright and godly lives in this present age, [13] while we wait for the blessed hope—the appearing of the glory of our great God and Savior, Jesus Christ, [14] who gave himself for us to redeem us from all wickedness and to purify for himself a people that are his very own, eager to do what is good.
—Titus 2:11–14

While We Wait

Dust puffs haloed my feet as I trudged up the dirt road. It was already Wednesday. If I didn't take care of things soon, it would be too late. My dad's words still echoed in my mind. He had left Sunday for his long-distance construction job and would be back at the end of the week. His orders were clear. I must do what he wanted by Friday, but I had already procrastinated for two days. Today had to be the day.

On Saturday I had said some mean words to a girl who lived at the other end of our street. Mindy (not her real name) and I were friends. Since kindergarten, we had played school, ridden bikes, and done whatever else two friends do when they are the only kids in the neighborhood. Now we were in third grade, and over the summer, some new kids had moved into the house across from mine. I befriended the newcomers and began spending more time with them and less with Mindy.

On that fateful Saturday, I was playing games with my new friends and showing off, as boys do, when Mindy rode by on her bike. Being full of myself at that moment, I thought it might be funny to yell something smart-alecky. Mindy did not see the humor in my remark. She raced back to her house and told her mother, who soon after phoned my parents. As I walked into the house later that day, my dad confronted me. After stalling some, I reluctantly confessed to the crime. He then sternly told me that I was to apologize to Mindy before he returned home on Friday. And so that Wednesday found me dragging my feet up the street to say my sorries before the arrival of the inevitable day of reckoning.

For me, this experience mirrors many of the features of Titus 2:11–14. Just as my week of decision-making and wary anticipation is lodged between my dad's departure on Sunday and his return on Friday, so also do these verses include in their midst a striking message about how we should live between the first and second advents of Christ.

The passage begins by declaring that God's saving grace "has appeared" for "all people"—it has "epiphanied," as the Greek says in verse 11. The first advent—which we celebrate on Christmas Day—is the manifestation of God's saving grace in Jesus. Skipping over the next verse for just now, we find we are to expect the "appearing [from the same Greek word] . . . of our great God and Savior, Jesus Christ"— and so we have the second advent. This is followed by an affirmation of the liberating work of Christ, purifying us to be a "precious people, zealous for good works" (v. 14, author's own translation).

Living soberly, uprightly, and godly lives will by default lead us to treat others according to God's ways.

Now getting back to the verse we skipped, verse 12—the one nestled between the two advent accounts—we come upon invaluable words, not about advent past or advent future, but about "the now age," as the Greek phrasing goes. We find that the saving grace of God is "training us" (RSV). The Greek word for "training" is used when teaching and disciplining children. What then follows is the purpose of this training. God's grace trains us "so that after renouncing godlessness and worldly desires"—that is, repenting of our rejection of God and our self-serving cravings—"we might live soberly and uprightly and godly" lives, in that order (author's own translation). Living "soberly" is about self-control and is the basis for living "uprightly," or in accord with God's ways, which then intensifies our devotion and closeness to God; ergo, we become "godly." The entire experience is transforming and leads to Christlikeness.

Much of this training boils down to relationship—that is, how we are to behave relationally, not only with God but also with others. Living soberly, uprightly, and godly lives will by default lead us to treat others according to God's ways. Loving God and neighbor is definitely in the warp and woof of these verses. But closely tied to this relational training is the expectation of Christ's reappearance. "While we wait," we are to be invested in this grace-infused training. There is a sort of deadline implied here. We are to take full advantage of this training and live it out now so that, at Christ's glorious appearing, he will find us faithful.

So how faithful was I to my dad on that Wednesday long ago? I obeyed. I apologized to Mindy—but with little zeal. And Mindy just shrugged her shoulders. But that Friday, when I reported to my dad, he was pleased. He knew, as I did later, that he had just given me a prep course in caring for others, preparing me in many ways for the message about grace we find in Titus.

—Richard Buckner

TUESDAY, DECEMBER 25, 2018

The Arrival of HOPE: Christmas Day

SCRIPTURE READING
Luke 2:1–20

¹ In those days Caesar Augustus issued a decree that a census should be taken of the entire Roman world. ² (This was the first census that took place while Quirinius was governor of Syria.) ³ And everyone went to their own town to register.

⁴ So Joseph also went up from the town of Nazareth in Galilee to Judea, to Bethlehem the town of David, because he belonged to the house and line of David. ⁵ He went there to register with Mary, who was pledged to be married to him and was expecting a child. ⁶ While they were there, the time came for the baby to be born, ⁷ and she gave birth to her firstborn, a son. She wrapped him in cloths and placed him in a manger, because there was no guest room available for them.

⁸ And there were shepherds living out in the fields nearby, keeping watch over their flocks at night. ⁹ An angel of the Lord appeared to them, and the glory of the Lord shone around them, and they were terrified. ¹⁰ But the angel said to them, "Do not be afraid. I bring you good news that will cause great joy for all the people. ¹¹ Today in the town of David a Savior has been born to you; he is the Messiah, the Lord. ¹² This will be a sign to you: You will find a baby wrapped in cloths and lying in a manger."

[13] Suddenly a great company of the heavenly host appeared with the angel, praising God and saying,

[14] "Glory to God in the highest heaven,
and on earth peace to those on whom his favor rests."

[15] When the angels had left them and gone into heaven, the shepherds said to one another, "Let's go to Bethlehem and see this thing that has happened, which the Lord has told us about."

[16] So they hurried off and found Mary and Joseph, and the baby, who was lying in the manger. [17] When they had seen him, they spread the word concerning what had been told them about this child, [18] and all who heard it were amazed at what the shepherds said to them. [19] But Mary treasured up all these things and pondered them in her heart. [20] The shepherds returned, glorifying and praising God for all the things they had heard and seen, which were just as they had been told.